ACKNOWLEDGMENT OF COUNTRY

We acknowledge and pay respects to the Custodians and Elders of Country. We thank them for allowing us to live, work on and visit their spiritual lands.

We thank our ancestors for their continued guidance and protection.

We also acknowledge the land on which you're on and ask that you be guided safely as you navigate your journey of being your best and chasing your dreams.

DEDICATION

This is for you.

This book has landed in your hands
for a reason.

Allow the words and love with which
it was written to ignite your passion
and purpose. If our words and messages
make a difference for just one person,
we will consider it a success.

We hope that one person is you.

CREATE

THE LIFE OF YOUR

DREAMS

IN YOUR

TEENS

A Motivational Guide to Unlock
Potential and Achieve Success

Kylie Captain   *Tyrell Johnson*

First published by Ultimate World Publishing 2023
Copyright © 2023 Kylie Captain

ISBN

Paperback: 978-1-923123-42-7
Ebook: 978-1-923123-43-4

Kylie Captain and Tyrell Johnson have asserted their rights under the Copyright, Designs and Patents Act 1988 to be identified as the authors of this work. The information in this book is based on the authors experiences and opinions. The publisher specifically disclaims responsibility for any adverse consequences which may result from use of the information contained herein. Permission to use information has been sought by the authors. Any breaches will be rectified in further editions of the book.

All rights reserved. No part of this publication may be reproduced, stored in or introduced into a retrieval system, or transmitted in any form, or by any means (electronic, mechanical, photocopying, recording or otherwise) without the prior written permission of the authors. Any person who does any unauthorised act in relation to this publication may be liable to criminal prosecution and civil claims for damages. Enquiries should be made through the publisher.

Cover design: Anna Gannon
Internal art: Michael Fardon
Layout and typesetting: Ultimate World Publishing
Editor: James Salmon

Ultimate World Publishing
Diamond Creek,
Victoria Australia 3089
www.writeabook.com.au

DISCLAIMER

This book contains the stories and opinions of the authors. They acknowledge that readers may have differing opinions and beliefs. Throughout the book, the authors use slang and or Aboriginal English which is different from Standard Australian English. The strategies used and suggested by the authors do not intend to replace professional advice or research.

CONTENTS

About The Artist   xi
Testimonials   xiii

PART A 1
Introduction   3
A Message from the Authors   13
Chapter One: Something Magical
   Happens When We Dream   41
Chapter Two: Exploring Career Options.
   You Can Be the First   89
Chapter Three: Breaking Cycles and
   Embracing Education   107

PART B 131
Quick Reads to Inspire and Motivate   131
Positive Affirmations   255
Dream Big Journaling Prompts   267
Acknowledgements   277
About The Authors   279

ABOUT THE ARTIST

Cover Design

Anna Gannon

Anna Gannon is a proud Wiradjuri Yinaa, born in Wagga Wagga – Wiradjuri Country.

"The colour blue, in different shades, signifies the learning and growth you will explore to establish your identity. The people, songlines and meeting places encompass all that is destined for you. The story in the 'dream' lettering represents all of the endless opportunities and the power you have to create the life of your dreams.

I am grateful for the wisdom of the Elders and knowledge holders who continue to guide and support me. Through art, dance, or weaving, I take time to slow down and fill my spirit, drawing inspiration from my culture and all around me. I see the world through my heart, not my eyes.

Internal Art

Michael Fardon

Campbelltown-based Aboriginal artist Michael Fardon holds a Bachelor of Visual Arts from the University of Western Sydney. Michael is a Dharawal man and self-taught artist who lives and works on Country using a range of styles and mediums, including painting and digital formats. Michael works closely with communities and schools to create collaborative mural art with Aboriginal students.

TESTIMONIALS

Jayden – 18

Thank you, Aunty Ky and Tyrell for believing in me and being positive role models.

I know this book will make a difference for many.

Prestan – 13

Every day is hard, but you have to put the work in to get to the next level and, by any means possible, keep going. Thank you, Aunty Ky and Tyrell for inspiring many of us to dream big and work towards our goals.

Aasha – 19

Growing up in the same community as Aunty Ky, it really shows that once you put your mind to something you can achieve whatever you want. All you need is that one person to believe in you. I have been fortunate enough to travel to places like Walgett, Goodooga and Moree with

Aunty Ky. I saw the impact of her work and the difference it's making. I am grateful for this opportunity to be inspired by the messages in this book. I highly recommend it to any teen who wants to learn practical strategies to dream big and create the life of their dreams. Thank you Aunty Kylie and Tyrell for writing this book.

Bobby – 17

Aunty Ky has shown me that you don't have to be a famous footy player, and that you don't need generational wealth to be successful in life. I've lived in the same flats Aunty Ky grew up in and to see where she came from to where she is now has inspired me to keep working towards my dreams and goals. Thank you Aunty Ky and Tyrell for writing this book and for inspiring so many of us to focus on our strengths and to dream big.

Testimonials

Savannah – 16

'Create the Life of Your Dreams in Your Teens' is a must read for every teen who is seeking inspiration and practical strategies to help them navigate challenges and tap into their full potential. Not only is it full of engaging stories and inspiration, it is full of short and easy to read information you can read in just a few minutes.

I am a 16-year-old business owner with big dreams. This book, and Aunty Kylie's previous book, 'Dream Big & Imagine the What If', have inspired me to back myself, dream big and work towards my dreams and goals.

I am striving the be the best version of myself and have many dreams and goals for the future.

A very big thank you to my mentor Aunty Kylie and her son Tyrell for writing this book, and inspiring me and the many others who will read it.

Rainey – 18

'Create the Life of Your Dreams in Your Teens' is both thought-provoking and inspirational. Learning about the lives and experiences of both Kylie and Tyrell has given me insight into the unlimited opportunities that lie ahead – not only for me but for everyone.

Being able to experience these glimpses of knowledge and advice has let me see what I have, and also what I dream to have, in a different light. Knowing that each and every person has the capacity to achieve their dreams and goals has inspired me to dream bigger and know that my aspirations in life can become a reality. Thank you, Kylie and Tyrell!

Mariah – 15

"Don't let the fear of judgement hold you back." The advice shared through this book has reminded me to trust and believe in the gifts that I have been blessed with and to block out the negative thoughts that may cross my mind.

Testimonials

"Express gratitude daily." I was reminded how important gratitude is in our daily lives. Kylie has shown me that gratitude can lead to happiness and happiness is success.

"Focus on progress not perfection." Reading this book has reminded me that there are different perspectives of progress and greatness. When you work hard and progress, there may be heartache and tears, however, it's important to keep going as it's all part of the journey.

As a young woman who is still navigating my teen years, Kylie has inspired me to work my way to living my dream and that it is more than achievable if I am patient, dedicated and willing. "If she can, so can I."

'Create the Life of Your Dreams in Your Teens' can be an eye opener, reminder or that bit of motivation you may need. This read will guarantee to leave you feeling happy, grateful and inspired.

Jorja – 14

"If you dream big enough anything can come true." This is just one of the many things I took out of this book. Being a teen myself, 'Create the Life of Your Dreams in Your Teens' has taught me to follow my own path in life and to not let anything stop me from my dreams and aspirations. This book has taught me the importance of setting goals, dreaming big, always trying new things and constantly learning in life. If you are given the opportunity to read this book, please grab it with both hands! Forever grateful, thank you, Kylie and Tyrell.

Steph – 13

I loved reading this book. It inspired me to dream big and focus on my strengths. When I go through challenges, I will open this book to remind me of my potential and that with hard work and dedication, I can achieve what I set my mind to.

Testimonials

Dillon – 16

I've never really read books before but surprisingly, I enjoyed reading this one. Thank you Kylie and Tyrell for sharing your knowledge and experience with us. I'll be sure to recommend it to my friends as we all need to hear the messages in this book. Thank you again.

Tia – 18

This story feels unedited, real and raw. Aunty Kylie and Tyrell are so genuine in their writing and have the ability to connect in a way that is very relatable and engaging. To know that someone can go through many difficult situations but not let that stop them from becoming another stereotype is what we need to see more of. Things are daunting when you go through your teens and become an adult. Having an almost step-by-step guide to help many of us be the best we can be is deadly and a total game-changer for us teens.

PART A

"Today a reader, tomorrow a leader."
 – Margaret Fuller

INTRODUCTION

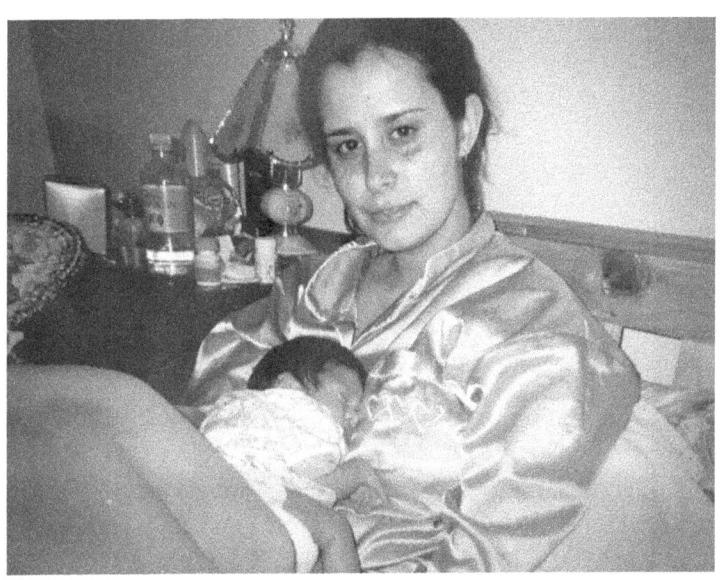

Holding her newborn baby, Kylie knew her son marked the beginning of a new chapter in her story. Life as she knew it would never be the same, and neither would she. From that moment, she decided that she would transform her life and be the best she could be.

Her love for her son and daughter, born four years later, empowered her to overcome the hardship and adversity she had faced with resilience and courage.

She often reflects on her past and wonders how things would have turned out if she didn't change her life. Those thoughts often scare her as the path she was heading down wasn't a positive one.

Kylie was pregnant at 18 and gave birth at 19. While her years prior were full of many memories to be grateful for, they were also filled with sadness, health issues, low self-esteem and grief from the passing of her mother when Kylie was a little girl. She became caught up in a cycle of pain, suffering and addiction and was heading down a negative path – a path that was scary and one full of uncertainty and heartache.

Introduction

Kylie's story and her determination to dream big and create the life of her dreams in her teens brought this book to life and is one of grit, determination, and hope.

This book was written in 2023 by Kylie and Tyrell – 23 years after Tyrell's birth!

As mother and son, they have been on quite the journey, and over the following pages they share their experiences about life and the little things that made a difference.

If this book has landed in your hands, there is a reason you are reading it. There may be a message you need to hear or even a reminder.

Teenage years are important.

You are becoming you.

Your identity and future are being shaped.

This time in your life is exciting, and can also be the most challenging. Your body is growing, your mind is expanding, there is so much to learn, so much to do – school, chores, homework, sport, responsibilities... the list goes on.

You're often told to wait till you're older, as that's when real responsibilities kick in and life really starts.

Some of that is true, however, it's in your teens when you discover who you really are and begin to set yourself up with the skills to journey through the exciting times and responsibilities that come with adulthood.

There is so much to learn at school, yet there's also so much you miss. Many 'real-life' skills and important things are sometimes left out of the very busy curriculum you are taught.

In this book, we write about all those little bits and pieces that will hopefully help you navigate this time in your life and support you to be the best version of yourself.

Over the following pages, we are going to share lots of different things – stuff around friendships, careers, social media, dealing with stress, becoming more organised and many other real-life lessons. We really did try to include so much without it being too overwhelming.

We went with our heart and added what we felt may benefit you.

This book is a combination of chapters and short, sharp bits and pieces that you can read in just a few minutes.

You don't have to read it from start to finish, you can turn to any page and find a little inspiration you need that day.

Reading this book may remind you that you're amazing and valued, or perhaps it'll give you a few tips to ignite your passion.

Whatever it is, we thank you for coming on the journey with us and allowing us to share in this special time in your life.

As we write this opening, we are away at a retreat, which has taken us away from the distractions of home and everyday life in order to allow the words we wish to share to land on these pages you are now reading.

Nestled in a treehouse cabin overlooking a billabong was an opportunity to reflect on how far we've come, and how truly blessed we are.

The last 23 years have been a roller coaster of ups and downs, happiness, sadness, challenges, ideas, inspiration, and new pathways. There have been tears and uncertainty, but one thing that has been constant is hope.

Hope to live a life of freedom and choice and to show up and be the best we could be.

To be writing a book as mother and son is a unique experience. We have gained an education and have the world at our feet. We can do as we choose and embark on a life and a career of our choice.

Time is precious, and we value the time that you put into your own self-care and navigating your way through this book, where we hope you will be taken on a journey. A journey of courage which we hope will lead you to creating the life of your dreams and living your best life.

We don't know it all, but one thing we know is that the power of our mind, thoughts and dreams can lead us to where we want to be.

Everything starts with a thought.

If your mind sees opportunities, go for them. Know that you are good enough and smart enough to do anything you set your mind to.

Work towards your dreams and goals. If you fail, there is always the opportunity to redirect and try again.

Set your intentions, live with gratitude, and show up with love in your heart and kindness for all.

Decide who is worthy of your time, absorb the knowledge and the wisdom from those around you, and those who inspire you, and importantly, never stop dreaming!

One moment is all you need to reset and ignite a spark within you. Commit to that moment and thought and give yourself a chance at your dreams.

We hope that you enjoy reading this book as much as we have enjoyed creating it for you.

We look forward to following your journey. We'll be cheering you on all the way.

Remember, if someone else can do it, then so can you!

Look back, only to see the progress you've made. Keep your eyes on the journey ahead.

Never be afraid to be different. You are special and unique.

Your future is waiting, so go get it.

We are proud of you.

All our love,

Kylie and Tyrell xx

Introduction

> "Nothing is impossible, the word itself says 'I'm possible'!"
>
> – Audrey Hepburn

A MESSAGE FROM THE AUTHORS

Kylie

You are the Author of Your Story

I'm sooo excited to connect with you! I know you're only a few words in but let me just say a massive yayyy!!

I am beyond thrilled to be connecting with you!

Writing a book alongside my son is a pinch-myself moment that I can't quite believe! Seriously!!

In July 2000, I became a mother. I was 19, scared and unsure, however I was ready to take on the world. I had no clue where I was going and what the future held for us.

We all have stories and unique experiences. We also share something in common – the ability to overcome challenges with resilience when we put our mind to it.

As a lifelong dreamer, my aspirations have shaped the success and freedom I enjoy today.

In this book, Tyrell and I will share yarns and information in the hope of inspiring you to dream big and be the best you can be.

I've walked the path from rock bottom to success, and I'm here to share these life-changing insights with you.

You're about to embark on an incredible journey, exploring 'what ifs' and hopefully unlocking your potential.

Remember, you're not alone on this journey.

As you explore, learn, and apply these messages, know that I'm incredibly proud of you.

A Message from the Authors

My world and life did take a miraculous turn, but it wasn't without the testing of my strength along the way.

My journey was once filled with obstacles and challenges. I was a disengaged student and found myself heading down a very negative path.

I've experienced unimaginable sadness and challenging health issues, but thanks to the support and belief of a teacher and my own grit and determination, I chose a different path, a path of freedom and choice. I embraced education, became a teacher myself and went on to work alongside principals and teach other teachers and leaders about my passion and commitment to Aboriginal education and making a difference in the lives of many.

From a little girl who grew up in public housing, I have achieved things that seemed way out of my reach.

I have travelled to incredible places around the world, graduated from uni, built my dream home, and become a successful author, speaker, and business owner.

I've always said that if someone else can do it then so can I, and I'm here to tell you that you can too!

We don't usually hear about quiet achievers like me, but there are many, and I dream that you, too, will go on and achieve whatever your heart desires.

I strive to empower others to transform their own lives, hence the reason for writing this book, and who better to write it with than my son. (I hope my daughter will write with me one day too... hint, hint 😊).

23 is my favourite number as my life changed for the better on the 23rd of July 2000 when I became a mother. Tyrell just so happens to turn 23 the year we publish this book. The timing and energy surrounding this book is incredible. I always go with my gut and do what feels right and let me tell you, this feels sooo right.

A Message from the Authors

I live my life by showing up and hoping to make a difference.

I hear from people all around Australia and overseas telling me the difference my books, journals and workshops have made.

We will all experience life differently. One thing we all have inside is hidden grit and resilience to tap into and use when needed.

For as long as I can remember, I have been a dreamer. There are a lot of things that are out of our control – tragedy, stress, difficulties at home, issues with friends, not getting that job, or achieving the outcome we want at school or on the sporting field. All of that is just stuff that happens in life – things may not always go our way.

One thing that we can control is how we respond to these events, which is why the power of positivity and having a strong mindset is so important.

Are you thinking of a change that you want to work on? Or perhaps you need a little inspiration to get back on track.

I encourage you to reflect on where you are and, importantly, what you are prepared to do to achieve your dreams and goals.

I am honoured to connect with you and share my experience of creating the life of my dreams in the hope to help you work towards yours.

As you read on and give some of our suggestions a go, I'm confident that you may truly unlock your potential – that potential that is waiting for you to tap into.

Once you know these things, you can't unknow them. They will be here to use throughout your life.

I wish you an abundance of health and happiness and whatever else you dream of.

You have everything you need to achieve your dreams – it starts with you.

A Message from the Authors

As I share my experiences and reflect on my journey so far, I want to make one thing clear – I haven't figured it all out.

I've simply learnt some deadly strategies along the way that have helped me navigate life's challenges.

Just like everyone else, I still have more to learn and areas in which I need to grow.

I encourage you to take the time to build up your own bank of strategies for when times get tough. Whether it's mindfulness, exercise, or talking to a friend or mentor, having a toolkit of techniques that work for you can make all the difference in difficult times.

Follow your heart and tap into your strengths.

You are unique, and you have something valuable to offer the world.

Don't be afraid to dream big and pursue those dreams with passion and determination.

The journey of self-improvement is a lifelong one.

I encourage you to embrace education, strengthen your resilience, and find your passion as you navigate your own unique journey of growth from your teens into adulthood.

Whatever you do, do it well and go hard.

Importantly, dream big... really BIG!

You never know unless you try. Imagine the 'what if' – like "what if she's right?" or "what if I really committed to my dreams and 'what if' they came true?"

I know you can do it and I'm here cheering you on all the way.

You've got this!

Lessssss gooo!

A Message from the Authors

Tyrell

My 'Why' and Experiences

I'm grateful for the opportunity to join my mum in co-authoring this book with the hope that you'll find valuable information and advice that may help you through the journey of your teens and life beyond.

If you have heard about my mum and read her previous books, you will know that she built her life from the ground up. She was a little girl who lost her mother at a young age, experienced grief and health issues and grew up very poor and still, somehow, she became the creator of the life she desired. She transformed her life to the point where she now has multiple properties, attained a university degree, authored multiple books, travelled the world, and creates new business partnerships seemingly every week. Her success continues to multiply.

Every time I see my mother, she has some exciting new opportunity to share with me (when I say every time, I mean *every* time, multiple times a day... yes it can sometimes get a bit annoying).

She allowed herself to dream her big dream. She acted as if there were no limits to her abilities. She got excited about the possibilities, and through her actions, she moved in the direction of achieving those dreams.

I remember before we moved into our 'number 21' dream house, I caught her sitting on a step with her eyes closed hugging her knees, face towards the sky, tears streaming down her face.

She was dreaming of the happiness she'd have once we owned that house. Visualising me and my sister swimming in the pool, watching TV with the glistening chandelier three or four metres above, parking her car in the garage and leaving for work in the morning.

I'm grateful for Mum, and I'm proud of her for all she has and continues to achieve, but enough about her, let's get to the good stuff.

What is my 'why'?

A Message from the Authors

My why is to help people and continuously improve myself. I've explored a few different careers and have learnt a lot throughout my time. I aim to use my experiences to create positive change.

In addition to writing this book, I also help Aboriginal people build wealth through property investment. Through my role, I guide people to create generational wealth which will allow them to have a higher standard of living for their future retirement as well as life in general. I also facilitate workshops based on financial literacy, dreaming big and creating the life that you desire.

Even though I'm only 23, I've managed to cram a lot of different experiences into my life. As I've grown, I've discovered that when you look back, there are some moments that stand out above the rest. Moments that make you feel proud. There are also other moments filled with grief and overwhelm. Naturally, I want to create an overall more positive experience of life. I paid attention and tried to figure out what these moments were made up of.

When I was at school, I would always say things like "why are we learning about geography and not things that we will actually use in life." Some of the subjects of this book are what I wish I had learnt at school. Don't get me wrong, I learnt essential skills and new ways of looking at the world, but not much that taught me about how to navigate the "real world".

Throughout this book, my mother (famous best-selling author and business owner, Kylie Captain) and I (her son still living at home), will break down how to lead a positive life and get through tough times.

As for the positive experiences I mentioned – those proud moments that make you feel good – my top three, in order, are:

1. Assisting a student that I was working with to overcome severe anxiety.
2. Building a house in one of the most disadvantaged areas in Peru for a family in need.
3. Completing a 6-month mixed martial arts program with zero lazy days off.

They really are the proudest moments of my life. Thinking of them brings an overwhelming sense of fulfilment and meaning to my life. They make the beating of my heart feel intentional.

As you might have noticed, two of these experiences revolved around _giving_ to other people, one of them revolved around _doing/improving_ myself, and none of them revolved around _receiving_. Although I am grateful for all that I have received, they have never brought me true fulfilment.

Win or Learn

John Kavanagh, Conor McGregor's trainer, wrote a book titled "Win or Learn", which inspired me to share this story.

When I was 17, I decided that I was going to train in Mixed Martial Arts (MMA) for six months and wake up at five in the morning, five days a week to train and at the end of the program, I'd have a fight which was an opportunity to test the skills I learnt. Most importantly, I vowed to myself that I would have no days off. I didn't want to do it unless I gave it everything.

A week after I had decided on this plan, about five minutes from my house, the Australian Kickboxing Academy was signing people up for a five-month challenge to train at five in the morning, five days a week, and then you'd fight someone from another gym. I was shocked at how perfectly it aligned with what I wanted. It was everything but only a month shorter than my plan to train for six months.

I signed up and did exactly what I said I would do. I had zero lazy days off (except when my mother forced me to miss three days and go on a family trip together, and I also missed another day when I couldn't stop vomiting). If it was cold, I was up and at the gym. If I didn't sleep, I was up and at the gym. From what I remember, it was always cold and I was always tired.

Coach Jim told me I could also train in the afternoons if I wanted to, and that's exactly what I did. I trained morning and night, with no days off. It just so happened that the fights were pushed back one month, and the six months I said I would train for happened.

Maybe I should've been more specific in my original vision and added that I would win the fight rather than just have the fight. I got choked to sleep at the end of round one in front of my favourite fighter, Robert Whittaker (you can laugh). I didn't tap out because it felt like self-sabotage. I would either get out of the choke successfully or go to sleep.

Although I had lost the fight, I didn't feel like a loser. I had never felt more like a winner in my life. I trained hard for six months straight. I battled with my own mind and challenged myself more than ever before. In my mind, no one I knew personally would voluntarily put themselves through that. I had lost the battle against my opponent, but I had won the war against myself.

Peru

In Year 11, I was given the opportunity to go to Peru with a handful of teachers and students to meet with a Peruvian school and go into the most underprivileged area to build a house for a family in need.

I had the opportunity to meet people from the other side of the world and saw what life was like for the people living in the poorest place I've ever seen. They lived in houses that looked like they could be blown away at any moment.

Unlike in other places, the poorest people have the best view. They live at the very top of the hills because they have to walk all the way up the steep path to get to their house. There were skinny dogs laying around and the ground looked dusty and lifeless.

I made the mistake of bringing my privileged Australian ideas with me and thought these people must not work or have jobs. I was proven wrong when we started talking to a woman who lived almost at the top of the hill. Her makeshift house was about as big as a small caravan. She had the job of peeling beans for 14 hours a day.

A Message from the Authors

We were told that if the peel got under your nail, it would be almost impossible to take it out, and the pain would be the worst pain you'd ever felt in your life and here she was, peeling them by hand for 14 hours a day.

Her thumbs had changed shape and were slightly bent back and flat from the years she had done it. She looked as though she hadn't slept in weeks, but whenever she spoke to us, she always had a smile on her face. The woman had three children. One of them was bedridden and needed surgery, but she could not afford it. Around three times a day, she would fill a bag much bigger than her with the peeled beans. She'd then have to carry the full bag down the mountain. Throughout the whole day, she would make about $6.

This experience was humbling. It taught me perspective, and it gave me a strong desire to help.

We had to carry prefabricated wood walls up these skinny dirt tracks, avoiding the mini cliff edges and stray dogs along the way.

We also built a house for another family of five. After we were done, all the students said goodbye to the family and began walking away. My maths teacher, Mr Maher, said "Boys, stop! Stop for a second and look over there," pointing at the house. "Look at what you have just done. That may have been a few hours work for you guys, but for that family in there, that was a once in a lifetime experience. They are so grateful for what you guys have done, and they will remember that moment for the rest of their lives."

I'm glad Mr Maher stopped us that day to reflect. It made me realise that one, I was lucky to live in such a high standard of living, and two, I have the privilege of being in a place where I can help people. That trip to Peru was life-changing. The memories, families and students we connected with will remain with me forever. The lessons I learned have stuck with me ever since.

Proudest Achievement

I worked as a School Learning Support Officer for three years. I won't go into details about

A Message from the Authors

the student or the situation, but it truly is the proudest moment of my life. I was able to assist someone younger than me to act with courage and slowly, over time, watch them as they worked through chronic anxiety and improve, day by day, week by week, until eventually, I was no longer needed. I saw them develop from someone paralysed by fear to someone with their confidence and inner power completely restored.

My only role was to assist, encourage and let them know that I was there, and that I was on their team. I could not force them to be courageous in the face of adversity. They did that themselves. This will also be the case for you.

Through my writing, my role is only to assist, encourage and let you know that I am on your team. I want you to experience the best that life has to offer, and when you face adversity or some metaphorical monster that you're not sure you can overcome, I want you to act with courage and persevere.

I want you to keep on learning. Keep moving towards fulfilment (if you don't know what you find fulfilling, I'd recommend the helping people and improving yourself path). Dream a big dream. Get excited about the idea and move towards it through your actions.

What's the worst that could happen? You don't reach your goal? You learn. It's okay if your life and your plans re-direct along the way.

I hope this book provides you with a blueprint and strategies to assist you in your endeavours. These are just a few experiences that stand out for me and things that have shaped me into who I am.

There are many things I am working towards in my life. I don't just set my goals, I create a plan on how I'm going to get there too.

Think about the things you're interested in or passionate about. You may not know yet. Hopefully by taking the time to reflect, you may begin to find your passion and purpose.

It's important to know there are steps and processes you can follow for setting, working towards and achieving your goals.

See the example below of some simple steps you may want to implement along with "Bob's" example.

Step one: What is your end goal and why do you want it?

Everyone wants success, but everyone has a different definition of what success means. What do you want for your future? And I don't want some basic, superficial or materialistic answer like, "I want freedom", or "I want a GTR". Be specific.

What do you want your life to look like?

Who do you want to be?

If you looked back on your life, what do you want to see?

Just as an example, I'll use something that everyone wants to some degree – money.

If we all want money, it's important to think about why we need it.

Let's use Bob as an example. Bob wants to be successful because he wants to spend as much time as possible teaching and raising his future children with his future wife. He also wants to be able to take care of his extended family, and beyond that, he wants to help others achieve peace, joy and fulfilment. Bob wants to own a house for his family to live in. To be more specific, he wants to have a lot of space outside for his kids to run around, and he wants a nice garden and a pool.

On top of this, he wants to have enough money to be in a place where he can afford to spend time with his family to make memories. For this, he requires money. Let's get specific and say he needs $100,000 dollars a year to live comfortably.

Step two: Work backwards from your goal

How can Bob make $100,000 dollars a year and still have time to spend with his family? He will either need to create an income stream to get him that money every year – this could be by running a business and providing a high-paying service – or he could go to uni and become a teacher, and invest his spare income.

Whichever route he chooses, one thing is for sure – he needs to learn, have a plan and stay committed in order to achieve these things. It'll require effort. It may be tough, and he may not have it all figured out, but if his 'why' is big enough, he'll do whatever it takes.

Let's say Bob is 17 and about to go into Year 12, and he decides to go to uni to become a teacher and invest his spare income in property. Bob needs to finish school, get into uni, complete his degree and become a qualified teacher. In 2023, first-year teachers are making $85,000 per year. Bob did some research and asked around and figured out that he could work part-time in a support role at a school while he studies to start saving money to go towards his future financial goals.

Step three: Investigate and plan your next steps then take action

You don't need to see the whole path ahead. But if you see the next step, you can move forward. Bob's Plan:

1. Bob figured that he'd put some extra effort into his Year 12 studies. He spoke to his teachers, told them that he wanted to go to uni and asked for tips and advice (investigate). He planned his study schedule. He decided to spend a minimum of an hour per day studying (plan). He created a routine of getting home, taking out his books and doing an hour of work while he ate a snack (take action).

2. He emailed and called different universities and told them his plan and asked if there was anything he could do to bring him closer to his goal (investigate). He figured out that he could be pre-approved for his university course (plan). So he applied to a bunch of different universities (take action).

3. He still had to learn about how to invest in property. So he started researching and contacting different companies and organisations. He read and watched YouTube videos (investigate). He figured out that he'd need at least a deposit of $40,000 dollars to buy an investment property (plan). He began working as a casual at Maccas to begin this journey (take action). He worked about 15 hours a week and made roughly $230 a week. If he could save 90% of that, he would have more than $10,000 dollars in his account within a year.

The point to take away here, is that once you have figured out where you are and where you want to be, you can start planning and taking action towards your goal.

I've shared information about setting goals and having a plan to achieve them. It's important to note that self-limiting beliefs and low self-esteem may also pop up on your journey. Self-limiting beliefs are ideas you have of what's possible. Self-esteem is based on your opinions about yourself and believing that you are good enough to deserve what you want.

The information in this book is only helpful if you believe in yourself. You must believe that you can achieve anything you are passionate about and that you deserve what you want.

Don't be afraid to work towards your dreams. You will never know if you can achieve them unless you try. Every successful person you can think of, all those people you admire, were young people once upon a time, just like you.

If they can achieve their dreams, so can you.

My top tips:

- Keep on going, no matter what obstacles get in the way.
- Remember that could'ves, would'ves and should'ves don't count – just do it!
- Don't stay in the pit of regret.
- When you make decisions, you either suffer or accept the consequences of your actions – make decisions wisely.

A Message from the Authors

- Learn: If you don't learn, you're doomed to repeat the same mistakes.
- If your spirits are low and you feel defeated, then just try to take the best first step in the right direction, no matter how little.
- If your spirits are high and you are motivated, use that momentum and TAKE ACTION.
- Embrace understanding: everyone is going through something. Many people are going through a lot of suffering in their lives. Whether it stems from something that happened in their childhood, adulthood or just something they may struggle with daily. You have no idea what they are going through.
- Be kind. Help lift others up and try not to put people down.
- Investigate and plan: Take time to think things through so you can be productive and use your time wisely.

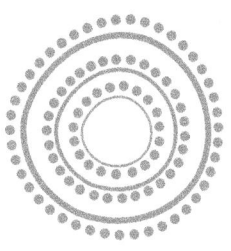

> "It always seems impossible until it's done."
> – Nelson Mandela

Chapter One

SOMETHING MAGICAL HAPPENS WHEN WE DREAM

Heyyyy guys, it's Kylie here. I thought I'd jump in and take you through this first chapter to set the scene and share some of my passion and experiences with you. Some of you may have heard me speak or participated in one of my workshops or even read my first book. If that's the case, hello again and if you're connecting with me for the first time, a very big hello to you.

We were meant to connect. I believe we connect with people for a reason. It could be for a moment, a chapter or a lifetime. Whether it's face to face, or in this case, even through a book.

In this chapter, I'm going to share a bit of my life and my 'why' with you. I shared some of this and much more in my first book. For the context of this book, I feel like I need to share some of my experiences, especially some of my teen experiences along with some of the challenges, success and strategies I've learnt along the way.

What you'll learn through this chapter, and from reading this book, is that I am a dreamer. I love to set goals and dream big, experimenting with lots of different things and exploring many of life's 'what ifs'. I love learning new things, exploring opportunities, and pushing boundaries to see what I can achieve. I've done many things that weren't meant for me, including exploring business opportunities, investing in property and travelling to incredible places around the world.

This is my third published book in three years! Like, what the?!

For years, I dreamt about writing one book, and here I am on book three. I have also stepped into running a successful business based on the themes of my books.

It all starts with a dream and two words that I absolutely love – 'what if'.

'What if' could spark imagination about the possibilities that await and that may also be our biggest regrets if we don't jump in and give ourselves the opportunity to explore the 'what if' in any areas of life.

There are also tonnes of books that have been written about dreaming big! In fact, I wrote one! It's called "Dream Big & Imagine the What If." "The Secret" is also one of my favourites.

For those who I'm connecting with for the first time, I'll share some of my story and experiences in this chapter, before Tyrell and

I take you through sharing lots of bits and pieces throughout the rest of the book.

Bob Proctor, a world-renowned speaker, motivational coach, and author of bestselling books, said, "If you can see it in your mind, you can hold it in your hand", and I believe this.

Everything starts with a thought.

You can close your eyes and visualise the outcome of the dream. Feel all the feels of what it would be like to achieve – that's dreaming!

There is no harm in thinking positively and working towards our dreams and goals, right?

They don't always work out, but you'll never know unless you try.

What's the worst that could happen?

You may not get there, or your dreams and actions may lead you down a different path.

Follow the signs and see where the journey takes you. People or events may come into your life just as you need them, and opportunities may begin to present themselves.

Continue to dream and visualise the outcomes you want, then keep an eye out for the signs.

Everyone has the ability to dream and it's important to understand that everyone's dreams are different and unique.

Many of the world's most incredible changemakers have dreamt their goals into reality.

Do some research and you'll start to notice that there are people who you know and follow who dream up and visualise their dreams and goals in many areas of life.

Successful athletes often visualise winning before they've even run the race or played their game. They see it in their mind as if the win is already theirs.

Dreaming big is not just about attracting material things. The power of positive thinking can help us work towards improved friendships, better relationships, desired job outcomes, better grades, and so much more.

It's important to read this chapter with an open mind and really start to think about what it is that you want to dream up or what you want to change in your life.

It doesn't have to be perfect, and you don't need to know it all right now, but it's important to have some little goals to work towards to start with.

There is something that happens to our brains when we achieve our dreams and goals – no matter how small they may be. It gives us this beautiful hit of endorphins that makes us feel good.

Dreaming up your dreams and goals is not about living in a fantasy and it's not about living a perfect life either. It's about living your best life, finding your true potential, and doing the things you love. Life doesn't have to be hard, so let's work together to learn a few things that may take away some of the fear to help you become the best version of yourself.

Goal Setting

I love setting goals!

Having something to work towards, whether it's personal or material, gives me that fire in my belly. When things get tough, I try my best to have a positive mindset and keep working towards my dreams and goals.

I remember when Tyrell was participating in the Wimp to Warrior MMA program. He was the youngest participant at just 17 and in his last year of school. It was a six-month challenge where he would train for an hour and a half at 5:00 a.m. every morning before school. When he asked if he could participate, I was scared. But I wanted to support his dreams and goals. However, I wasn't sure if doing something like this during his HSC was a good idea. His goal was to go the entire time without missing a day. He set goals and wrote in his journal as if he had already achieved them. He wrote something like, *"I'm so happy that I've just completed this program. I went every single day for six months, with zero days off."*

He set his intention and his goal.

His dedication and commitment was inspiring. He went the entire time without missing a day. Their motto was "while they were sleeping", meaning while everyone else was sleeping, they were up, training and smashing out their dreams and goals.

Many people show commitment like this. It's incredible to see the dedication and motivation that is within them. We all have it. We just need to ignite the fire by setting our intention for what we want, then get serious about taking those steps towards achieving our goals.

We must remember, it's not all about having dreams; it's about taking action too. That's where the real magic is.

Break down your goals into simple steps and live in the moment. It's also important to practice gratitude for all you have. I believe that gratitude attracts more good things into our lives.

Here's a few of my top tips that you can practice every day to help bring joy, and hopefully, your dreams to life.

- Practice gratitude every day
- Journaling
- Set goals and visualise achieving them
- Surround yourself with people who uplift and inspire you.

Let's chase our dreams together and make this world a better place!

Imagining the What If

I was a kid who struggled and who has had to work hard to get to where I am, so dreaming big and lots of imagining the 'what if' has led me to where I am.

I would often think, *"what if I could really do that"*, or *"what if I could get that job"* or travel to those incredible places. Everything I've achieved started with the same question – 'what if?'

So, who am I anyway, and what gives me the authority to write a book like this?

You'll learn more about me as you go on but here's a little snapshot in case you were wondering.

I am a proud Gamilaroi author and educator. I am a homeowner, a teacher, a business owner, a world traveller, a property investor and I'm just me 😊.

I have experienced a lot of sadness from losing many loved ones, including my birth mum, when I was just a little girl. I also lost other close people in my life, including my mum who raised me. (I was lucky to have my Aunty become my mum when my mum passed away). Sadly, I also lost my nan, my sister, a best friend and even the father of my children when they were little.

Grief and losing loved ones, or even pets, are such sad things to go through, and are also at times very difficult to overcome.

There are many stages you go through with grief and there are times when we need to seek the help of counsellors or support people to help come to terms with what has happened and how to build strength.

Day by day, I kept moving forward, one step at a time. I knew there was always hope that things would get better with time.

Sometimes life feels like one big test, and sometimes it's not about how well you do, it's just about passing and hopefully having fun, and finding joy and happiness along the way.

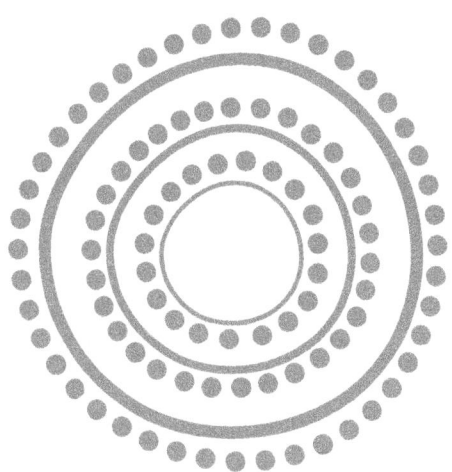

> "The beautiful thing about learning is that nobody can take it away from you."
> – B.B. King

My Teenage Years

My teenage years were tough. I missed so much school as I spent a lot of time in hospital with psoriasis, a terrible skin condition that covered me in thick, itchy, red scales. Specialists from all around the world would fly into Sydney to see my skin and I was used in many studies. It was sad as my self-esteem was low as I could never wear shorts and a t-shirt. Whenever I was in public, I would always be in trackies and long sleeves. Other kids from the hospital were unkind and would sometimes call me names or stare at me which made me feel insecure. I already knew something was wrong with me so having people stare or ask what it was embarrassed me. I hated it and prayed it would go away. Sadly, it didn't for a long time. It was as an adult when I started to find some relief and now I have it under control.

Growing up, I always felt like the least capable kid in the class. I was always behind and didn't know much. At school, I would get so anxious about learning and schoolwork. I wanted to be invisible. I never wanted the teachers to ask me any questions and I was very shy.

In my teens, I went down a negative path that was leading me to a lifetime of sadness and helplessness, and things started to spiral out of control.

Sadly, and something I'm ashamed of, is that I used drugs, would binge drink and shoplift for basic necessities. I'm not proud of these things. I'm sharing this with you to demonstrate that you can go through hard times and still achieve your dreams and highlight the devastating impact these choices had on me. I was sad, scared and very much alone within my mind, suffering through my teens. I wish I could turn back time and tell myself that everything would be okay and to be kind to myself and keep asking for the help I needed.

I really was lost. I didn't have any dreams and I was living day by day. I was trying my best to numb the sadness and pain, however something within me kept telling me to follow the signs and keep showing up with kindness in my heart. I was always polite and kind. I think those qualities helped me a lot in life. In fact, they still do today. Think about it, do you like helping people who are mean, rude or ungrateful? I doubt it. Kind and nice people are a joy to be around. Their energy is warm and feels like sunlight – that's who I want to be and the type of people I like being around.

As we publish this book, I am now 42 and my children, Tyrell and Allira, are 23 and 19.

Something interesting about me is that I have what they say is a life-threatening heart condition (I believe my heart is strong and amazing 😊). This condition, and near-death experience in my teens, required me to have an Internal Cardiac Defibrillator (ICD) – an electrical box that sits within my chest. Wires are screwed within my heart, and it's there to help keep me alive and safe. If my mum had one of these devices, it may have saved her.

I'm grateful for life.

I often joke and say that I'm like an Energizer Bunny – I just go, go, go! Writing books, running a business, holidaying in beautiful places and always dreaming up new and creative ideas.

I'm always wanting to be the best version of myself.

I refuse to let tragedies or circumstances dictate my path.

People often use the term "these are just the cards I've been dealt", assuming that this is the life they were destined for and find it hard to visualise another path. I turn that saying around and do the opposite. I keep throwing the cards back until I have a nice hand that I'm happy to play – one that I've dreamt up and intentionally created.

Growing up, I lived in the inner-city suburbs of Redfern and Waterloo. I lived in public housing for the first 26 years of my life and didn't have much. I didn't ever see myself leaving Waterloo, unless it was to go to Walgett, which we did a lot when I was a kid. I loved travelling back and forth, however there was a lot I didn't see. What I missed were the opportunities and role models who were doing incredible things. I didn't know that Aboriginal people could be successful in the areas that I have succeeded in.

I never had the opportunity to participate in extracurricular activities like dancing or sport. Things like that were not available to me, nor was the life I'm now living.

Being an author of three books is an achievement that I am so proud of as I've worked hard to get to where I am.

I never thought I'd achieve things like building my dream house, which has four levels and everything I have dreamt of and more. You name it... a beautiful big pool, spa, home theatre, and all the fancy things that the rich and famous have.

I have travelled to many incredible places in Australia and around the world. Places like Disneyland, Las Vegas, The Bahamas, Canada, Florida, New Zealand, Thailand, Bali, Fiji

Greece and others. I still have lots of places I'd love to visit as I love the memories that travelling provides.

I decided to dream big and take life into my own hands.

Never in a million years did I think I could live the life I currently live. We hear of these experiences and opportunities from our sporting stars or famous singers that make it big.

You can achieve just as much by doing what you love, and it doesn't have to be in front of the cameras, climbing your way to the top through fame and fortune.

A big part of my story is about the power of education and a teacher believing in me.

That's why I became a teacher. I wrote my second book with my teacher and still work alongside her. I even teach her new things now.

I am now also a new business owner.

My business is called Dream Big Education Wellbeing & Consulting where I facilitate inspiring student programs, teacher masterclasses and Aboriginal cultural capability training.

I also speak at events all around the country and have even started receiving invitations to speak at events internationally.

I still pinch myself and wonder how I got here.

After the tragic loss of my fiancé when my children were little, I didn't think I would ever find love again. That was one of the saddest parts of my story, and again, I stood strong in the face of adversity and carried on.

I now have an incredible husband and I'm forever grateful for the opportunity to find love again. His upbringing was similar to mine; he grew up not having much.

One of the things I love most is being a mum. I am so proud of my kids. They both went on to get an education and now also live a life of freedom and choice – exactly what I hoped for them. They are now adults who know how to navigate life and the world. I feel like I've done the best I could do with what I had. I'm proud of the way they've navigated the ups and downs of life and their own grief and hard times.

I love my kids more than anything in this world.

Tyrell has always been a wise young man. I go to him with lots of big ideas and he always has great advice.

As much as I am proud of my son, I'm equally proud of my beautiful daughter Allira.

Allira is my best friend – like seriously! We laugh and go on silly together. She's a lot like me and so many people say she looks just like me (sometimes we see it).

I am grateful for all of my experiences all the challenges as well as the tremendous success I have had.

I have this desire to share the messages that I've learnt over the years with people like you in hope for you to achieve your dreams and goals.

Do I know it all? No way! All I know is that from my experience and through challenging times, it's easy to get stuck in a cycle of negative 'what if' thoughts.

Your worrying thoughts might take you from, "What if it doesn't go well?" or "What if something bad happens?" to "What if I never get out of this situation?" When you are trapped in this cycle of thinking, you can feel hopeless.

I try to flip those 'what if' thoughts on their head and instead imagine them in a positive light.

Completing a University Degree

Completing a university degree is not something that I ever thought I was capable of achieving. I always thought that you had to be rich and smart to go to university, and that certainly wasn't me.

I didn't really know people who went to university, and I was told that the academic reading and writing was hard.

Even though I knew it was going to be a big challenge, I still had something inside me wondering if I could do it.

I always wanted to become a teacher.

As soon as I left high school, I was offered placements at three universities. I accepted an offer to study at the University of Sydney. That didn't last long. I didn't have the money or resources to succeed, and I didn't try to problem solve and work out how to overcome some of those barriers. Life was tough at that time. I decided to quit and fell back into negative habits.

However, I magically landed a job at the Department of Aboriginal Affairs a few months later – a job I dreamt about in my teenage years. The Hon. Linda Burney, MP, was the boss there at the time. She interviewed me and offered me the job on the spot. That was a moment that also changed my life as there were many jobs I had applied for and no one wanted to give me an opportunity.

When I was working at the Department of Aboriginal Affairs, I fell pregnant with Tyrell. I was 18 and suffering from severe morning sickness. I decided to leave my job and stay home to focus on my health for the rest of my pregnancy. This was only a year or so after a terrifying near-death experience caused by my binge drinking, which triggered dangerous heart rhythms, causing me to black out – an experience I don't like to recount as my doctor says he doesn't know how I survived. I'm glad I made that decision to take care of my health first.

I was a stay-at-home mum for the first two years of Tyrell's life. His dad and I did a good job as young parents. I focused on being a mum and learning how to take care of myself so I could be the best mum I could be.

I then decided to apply for a job at St George Bank where I spent the next six years and was quickly promoted to a specialist position. I absolutely loved my time working there.

There are many jobs we can do without a university degree. I could've quite happily stayed at the Department of Aboriginal Affairs or St George Bank, but I wanted more. I knew I wanted to be a teacher and those earlier years of dropping out of university were always on my mind. I kept thinking 'what if' and I kept thinking about my teachers and support staff who made a difference for me. At school, I also had Aunty Linda and Uncle Hilton who were always there as a friendly face, and people I knew I could go to if needed. I know there are many support staff who do incredible jobs. Aunty Deb and many others show up and do such an amazing job for our students.

You may have your own special someone who comes to mind.

I love children, and I remember someone saying to me that it doesn't feel like work if you do what you love, so for me, embarking on a job in teaching or working with children would be a win-win situation. I could work with young people and make a living.

Fast forward quite a few years, after my time at St George, I landed a job where I worked in community services, helping vulnerable families. I got this job just before the sudden and tragic passing of the kids' dad (the hardest and saddest thing I have ever experienced). I don't know how I did it, but here I was working in a challenging job where I was helping vulnerable families, yet I was in such a vulnerable situation too. I did my best and loved helping other families. Helping others helped me stay focused on helping myself, too.

I then went on to work in education, but not in a teaching role. I was working as an attendance officer, supporting students who had attendance concerns. I was also supporting their families who needed extra support to manage some of their problems to prioritise the attendance and education of their children. This is a job that I loved and had so much success doing.

I get these thoughts and feelings that just won't leave me until I dive in and do it. I kept getting ideas about university. I didn't know how I was going to do it because I had a full-time job where I was already making pretty good money, and I had a mortgage, so I needed to work full-time. I also had two young children who were busy with sports, dancing, and everything else that comes with being a mum – cooking, cleaning, and still trying to be the fun aunty and having my nieces and nephews over when I could.

My teacher, Ms Burgess, was always a great support, and I decided to email her. I wanted to know what she thought about the possibility of me working full-time, studying full-time and raising my two young children. I knew it would be a massive challenge and one that scared me. I was scared because I didn't want to embark on something only to fail – something that we will all experience. Fear of failure is real and often holds us back because we all want to succeed.

I decided to be brave and take action towards this possible dream.

I emailed Ms Burgess and said something like, "Hi Ms Burgess, I hope you're well. It's been a while between emails, but I wanted to ask your advice. Since leaving Clevo all those years ago, I still have this dream of going to university and becoming a teacher. The only thing is that now, I have extra responsibilities. I am working full-time, raising my two young children and have a busy social life with taking them to things like sports and dancing as well as family commitments, etc. I am wondering if I can do it all? It means that I would have to work full-time, study full-time and do all those extra things because I need to work as I have a mortgage now."

After writing her a long email, she responded with a very short sharp and to the point response.

She said, *"You're smart, you can do it."*

She gave me the answer I was looking for, even though it terrified me.

I decided to apply for university. I went to sit for the required testing and was offered a place to study. It all seemed to happen fast. I took that action and worked towards my dream.

I'm very lucky that I worked for a supportive workplace and had access to study leave. I worked extremely hard over the next four years, studying most nights, going into the uni on the weekend, and putting extra hours into my studies.

I still remember my first day going to uni. I felt terrified. As I walked in, I said a little prayer to the heavens above/God/my mum/my nan – anyone who was out there. I prayed for them to give me the words, the brains, the motivation, and dedication to stay committed to my studies.

Because I was so busy, things were tough at times. I didn't like academic writing as I've always felt that I had the answers and the ideas, and I often questioned why I needed to reference somebody else who had those same thoughts or ideas – that stuff annoyed me.

I got a tutor to help me learn how to reference and structure my work academically. I picked it up quickly and didn't need too much support. I just needed someone to show me, as that's how I learn. I can read things from a textbook; however, if you show me, I will learn 10 times faster. That's what I did. I asked for guidance, reached out to those around me for support and chipped away, subject by subject, semester by semester. Eventually, I got to the end of those four years and graduated in front of my children and husband. That was one of the proudest moments of my life.

Uni was a great experience. I made lifelong friends and had such an amazing time. There is so much support now for young people. The Badanami Centre at Western Sydney University was incredible. The lecturers and support staff were excellent. A special shout out to Dr Les, Jan and Alison, who supported me throughout my course. They provided me with all the support and guidance we needed. Importantly, what they did was believe in me. I had many wonderful lecturers over those four years, and I learnt so much about life and my abilities to achieve.

I was averaging distinctions and high distinctions which landed me on the Dean's Merit List for my academic achievement – that's something I'm pretty proud of. I even got to travel to Canada as part of my studies! How good is that! It was amazing!!

My message to you here is to believe in yourself. Don't let fear hold you back. Always remember that if someone else can do it then so can you.

There are supports and people out there that can help. If you don't feel like you have the skills to achieve academically, reach out for help. There are people employed in these jobs to help people like you and me.

University doesn't always have to be the end goal.

You can achieve just as much success or fulfilment in life doing whatever it is you like.

Throughout this book, we encourage you to think about the things you enjoy, the things you're good at, and hopefully, as you progress, start to gain confidence, and stand taller, stand prouder and really tap into your potential.

You will never know unless you try.

My Dreaming

As I grew up and faced challenges, the question of 'what if' kept coming up for me. I never thought I was good enough to do anything and to be honest, didn't even have anything in mind that I wanted to work towards as there were no seeds planted in my mind about the possibilities.

Eventually, I started having dreams after I was exposed to people and things that inspired me. I started believing I was capable and smart enough to work towards that dream, just like anyone else.

My dream was to be a mum, get a job and hopefully have a house with a pool. It might not sound like a big dream, but it was to me.

And you know what? I achieved all of my dreams and more. I have my dream house with my pool, plus much more! I worked hard and believed in myself, and I ended up going on to achieve beyond what I thought was possible.

I started seeing myself as someone with knowledge that I should share with others. It became important for me to pass on what I learned to help others believe in their potential and chase their dreams.

I don't achieve every single goal I set. Many dreams don't turn out the way I expect them to. But I see those moments as opportunities for growth and learning. There's always a lesson to be learned from dreams that don't come true.

Dreaming big and visualising has supported everything I've achieved in life. It's not something new; it has been used by incredible scientists and changemakers throughout history. Essentially, it's just about having goals and attracting positive things into your life through your thoughts, energy and of course the work you put in.

It's about living a positive life, visualising what you want to achieve, and seeing your thoughts and energy as magnets.

The power of positive thinking can be life changing – it certainly was for me. It encourages us to flip our negative thinking to having a positive outlook. Many of us limit ourselves to what we *believe* we deserve.

Overcoming limiting beliefs isn't easy and takes effort. I haven't mastered it all, but I know that when I commit and put my mind to it, it usually works in my favour. If it doesn't, then there is always a lesson to learn through the process.

To visualise and achieve success, we must first believe that anything is possible.

Visualise the outcomes you want and truly believe that you can achieve them. Focus on abundance and happiness and engage in positive experiences that align with your thoughts.

Gratitude is also a vital part of dreaming big.

I practice gratitude every day, giving thanks for even the smallest things in my life. As I wake up in the morning, I say thank you for every blessing in my life.

The first step is to become a dreamer and learn to create visions and movies in your mind.

Believe that your desired outcome is already yours and imagine the thoughts and feelings you will have when you achieve it.

I really do believe in the power of visualisation and have even brought myself to tears while visualising my goals as if they were already mine.

I encourage you to give it a go and see what happens.

I've worked hard to attract the things that I have achieved and experienced. I refuse to sit back and wait for life to happen.

I have dreamt up many things in my life and I'll continue to use this practice for the rest of my life.

Let me share a yarn about buying my first home in 2009 and then my dream house in 2016.

These were our previous homes. We ended up going on to build our second dream home which we moved into at the end of 2022.

Our new home is incredible. The dreams keep getting bigger and bigger. I wish I could switch it off sometimes as my brain is always dreaming up new things to work towards, not just material things but lots of different things. New skills I want to learn, health improvements – that is a massive one for me as it's a constant battle to stay consistent with eating well and exercising. If I fail or get off track, I always jump back on and keep working towards my little goals.

As I write, I just picked up my first luxury car too. I am not really a car person, but I think it was time to part with my seven-seater mum car and get something a little smaller and oh em gee... it's flash as! It has all these buttons and fancy things I don't even know how to use yet. It can even park itself and I can move it with the key like a remote-control car. LOL.

Anyway, back to the yarn I was telling you about the 2009 and 2016 dream home.

After working at St George Bank for six years, helping lots of customers buy homes, I had a dream to be on the other side of the counter.

I didn't know any other Aboriginal people who owned a home. I only thought that I could apply for a housing commission place and hoped that I might be given a house with a yard, as I'd lived in a unit all of my life.

I was going through a hard time. I was living in community housing where I was very comfortable. I could have stayed there and had the security of my rent going up and down depending on my wage, but I really wanted to buy a home. I had money in the bank and was good at saving, so I set my self some goals. I knew what I needed to do to make it happen from my experience working at the bank. It was just having the courage to do it. It meant signing up for a large loan on my own, which would force me to work hard so I could afford to pay my mortgage, and that's exactly what I did. I purchased our first home, and it was one of the proudest moments in my life. And I did it as a single mum.

I still smile with pride as I recall getting approved for my home loan, and importantly, taking those first steps into our new home.

I encourage everyone to work towards the goals of home ownership and I'm so proud that Tyrell now works in that space where he is not only working on his own property goals, but also helping many others too.

Along with that first home, we went on to buy other homes too and purchased our first dream home in 2016.

I knew this house was the one. It was like a house that celebrities and the rich and famous lived in. It was near new and was very fancy. It was like walking around in a five-star hotel; beautiful and very expensive.

It was number 21 (the one Tyrell referred to earlier), which is my wedding date, and as we entered the home for inspection, I noticed the same picture and cushions that we had in the house we were living in that said, *"If you dream big enough, anything can come true"*.

I was so excited from the moment I laid eyes on this house, and I knew it had to be ours.

I had this 'what if' moment and I wanted to try my best to make it happen. I wanted to try to achieve what seemed like an unachievable dream. I wanted to show my kids that we could achieve anything we set our minds to.

My husband and I didn't come from money, so we were way out of our comfort zone, even just thinking of buying this house.

The minute we walked through the door, I remembered a moment from my childhood where I ran into the glass door on the way to the pool of a house I was visiting. I had never been to a flash house like that before so the memory stuck with me. That moment also planted a seed for me, as I always remembered that pool, and would often think about how cool it would be to own a house and a pool like that.

As we walked in, I looked straight to the back where I could see a beautiful, sparkling pool. Everything was amazing, and all these signs letting me know that it was the one.

I broke it down into simple steps and took away the belief that this wasn't the type of house we should be buying.

I thought about what everyone else must do. They work, save money, qualify for a home loan, and then they reach out to the right people for support. So that's what I did.

It takes time, but things like this are achievable. I learnt these steps from working in the bank and seeing everyone else achieve their property goals. I saw the joy on their faces when they purchased their homes, and I wanted that, too.

Anyway, off I went. I was a woman on a mission, out to achieve the unachievable goal and buy this house.

I worked hard and did everything required of me to be approved for a home loan. I kept thinking "If someone else can do it, so can I".

I would imagine how I would feel if I achieved that goal. I would dream away as Tyrell mentioned earlier.

We did it, and again, I tested my strength to set and achieve massive goals. I followed the same steps from when I bought my first house in 2009.

We had an incredible six years living in that house, and had many beautiful summers swimming in the pool and enjoying all life had to offer.

It truly was a dream come true.

I never thought we would leave; however, after Allira finished her HSC, I realised we had a chance for a fresh start. Tyrell found us the perfect block of land where we built our next dream home, which we absolutely love. We took all the things we loved from our previous home and added them into our current home, plus all the extra things we thought would be cool, such as an even bigger pool with a spa and a theatre. We purchased a block of land on a slope and had to be creative with the design. It's actually built over four levels. We love it and have already had our first year here. We have the most beautiful sunsets from our home. Summers are the best, and I love being in the spa at night, looking up at the stars and expressing gratitude for everything in our life. Will we be here forever? Who knows. I often get my little inspired thoughts and ideas and run with them. Hopefully, one day, I'll have grandkids running around, filling my home with laughter because, to be honest, as much as I'm grateful for the incredible humans I've raised, I do miss little kids (hint, hint lol).

When dreaming big, you must remember that it's not all about dreaming it up, we need to take the steps to put in the work too.

I've dreamt up travel and lots of amazing experiences. The day after Tyrell graduated from Year 12, we were on a plane for a month-long trip around the United States. We went to Disneyland, Florida, The Bahamas, Vegas, Hollywood, Universal Studios, and much more. Again, this trip was part of my plan. I saved, I researched and importantly I believed my family could have an amazing trip like that and we did it.

So… you now have a bit of an idea about me and how my mind thinks about dreaming big and I hope that you, too, will start to set some goals and become a dreamer. Nothing makes me happier than to see others achieving success and breaking through barriers along the way.

If it's a job we want, we need to do what's required to work in that job. If it's making a sporting team, we need show up to training and be consistent. If we want a new phone, we need to save money and think of ways to make extra cash. Get creative and become an amazing problem solver and smash out your goals.

The dreaming part helps us stay motivated and committed to achieving the goal.

Next, I'll share a few steps to help you start to become a dreamer.

Becoming a Dreamer

Get clear and decide what you want.

Close your eyes, quiet your mind, and allow yourself to dream up the best possible scenario in any area of your life. Think about where you are now and where you need to be – whether it's finishing your current school year or doing well in upcoming exams. Visualise yourself achieving a little goal. See yourself jumping up and down and celebrating. That's where the real magic is.

Start to think about what you would do if there were no chance of failing.

Write it down, sit with your eyes closed, smile, and see yourself there. Believe that you can achieve whatever it is you want to do in life, whether that is being a singer, a famous author, an incredible business owner, travelling the world, living in a mansion, or volunteering your time helping the poor.

Really get into imagining.

All these things are not out of your reach – it starts with dreaming and by imagining the 'What if'.

Sometimes it's hard to see ourselves living our dreams because our upbringing or our current circumstances don't reflect what we're hoping to achieve.

What if you gave it a go and everything worked out?

There is something so magical about the power of dreaming and using our imagination, just like we did when we were children.

Dream it up!

Once you learn to use your imagination and imagine the 'what if', you may find that opportunities, experiences, and positive things just start to turn up and flow into your life.

Doors may begin to open, and you will feel more empowered to take positive steps to find your passion and purpose.

Find Your Dream Space

Find a space where you feel comfortable and can sit and dream uninterrupted. My space varies. Sometimes it is sitting out in nature whilst other times, it's in my lounge room, in bed – anywhere.

Start by taking some deep breaths and relaxing into your dream space. Say some positive affirmations like "I am safe", "I am good enough", or "I am a magnet for all good things". Positive affirmations have an incredible way of transforming our beliefs about our ability to achieve.

Here are some tips to dream about:

- ◉ Your dream career
- ◉ Your dream house

- Your dream car
- Your dream holidays
- Your dream pet
- Your dream friends
- Your dream health

Use the Dream Big Journal or reflection section in this book to get into the finer details about your dreams and goals.

Take a moment to reflect on your dreams.

How do they make you feel?

What steps can you take to work towards them?

By focusing on positive thoughts and feelings, we have the power to create our dreams and work towards our goals.

Setting clear intentions and working on our thoughts and feelings can lead us to attracting our dreams into our lives.

We need to remember to express gratitude for what we already have, as this will bring our mind to a place of positivity.

Tips for getting started are:

- Surround yourself with positive influences and rub shoulders with people you respect or people doing what you hope to be doing.
- Take inspired action and work towards your dreams and goals.
- Have a positive mindset.
- Practice positive affirmations.
- Be kind to yourself and others.

You've got this!

Now have a go with dreaming up your first little dream.

Turn to the back of the book where you'll find journaling prompts to get you started.

> "Whether you think you can or think you can't you are right."
> – Henry Ford

EXPLORING CAREER OPTIONS. YOU CAN BE THE FIRST

Have you ever taken the time to think about your career path and what you would like to achieve in life?

It's ok if that thought has never crossed your mind. Often, we don't think about these things until it's time to prepare for subject selection or coming towards the end of our schooling and need to decide where to go next.

It's never too early to start thinking about these things – to allow your mind to imagine the 'what ifs' and the many different career pathways that await.

You might go on a journey of exploring many different careers until you find your passion and purpose.

You don't have to do what everyone else does, you could be the first!

Sometimes when we think about what we want to be, we look in our own homes, or within our immediate community, to explore what possibilities are there for us.

Don't think that because people in your own family or community are not doing the things you would like to do, that these things are not available to you.

We encourage you to start thinking about what you enjoy. There are many different things that we can do to find out what our passion is. Sometimes it's a little tricky to work it all out, but you don't have to know it all right away – there is time to explore.

Kylie

I've have had the opportunity to work in many different jobs. I didn't land my dream job right away. We have to start somewhere and build on our skills.

I remember feeling inspired and motivated to try to make a positive change in my life.

I applied for a job at a large bank in the city. I was excited and nervous when I went to my job interview. I will never forget that experience and how sad the hiring manager made me feel.

He looked at my address and realised that I lived in Waterloo. He made me feel worthless. He humiliated me by judging me and making me do tests without even looking at my results before telling me the job wasn't for me. He left me feeling like I was never going to be good enough. I was angry with myself for even thinking I could work at a fancy bank, as I was just a teen from Waterloo with no hopes for the future (well that's what he thought, and to be honest, so did I). If anyone would have told me that I'd be doing all the things I'm doing now, I honestly would have laughed and told them they were dreaming lol.

I decided that I would not let him win. That experience made me want to work harder to prove him wrong, and as I sit and write my third book and look around at all I have achieved, I think it's fair to say I did prove him wrong and, importantly, I proved to myself and everyone else that we are the writers of our future. We get to choose which path we take, who we hang out with, the choices we make and who we reach out to for support. Our future and life really is in our own hands.

Don't let the negative energy or lack of belief from others stop you from being the best version of yourself. Life is meant for living and there are so many amazing things to do, achieve and experience if you want them.

Have you ever had an experience where someone's negative thoughts, words or energy stopped you from moving forward with your goals?

I encourage you to dig deep and prove them wrong.

The most important person who you need to prove anything to is you.

Make yourself proud.

I went on to have many different jobs throughout my career.

My first job was at Woolworths. I had applied for a few other jobs, however, I never heard back from anyone which left me feeling disappointed at times. I remember how scared I was when I went for my interview. My starting salary was $5.62 an hour and I was very much out of my comfort zone. Thankfully, after many failed attempts, someone finally said yes and gave me an opportunity.

I had to talk to people, learn new things and allow myself to be vulnerable. But I quickly realised that there was a lot for me to learn in this job. It provided me with the stepping-stones and tools I needed to learn and grow.

I was a customer service assistant which basically meant I was a checkout chick. I learnt customer service, money handling, conflict resolution and how to deal with unhappy customers. I really enjoyed working there. I also enjoyed the mundane tasks of stacking shelves and unpacking deliveries. For the first time in my life I was making money and it felt so empowering.

From there, I went on to have a few other jobs. I worked at Burger King for a while and started a traineeship at the Department of Aboriginal Affairs, before landing my first long-term job which was at St George Bank. I worked at St George Bank for six years and was quickly promoted to a specialist position. Those skills that I learnt from Woolworths, Aboriginal Affairs and Burger King really helped me in my Customer Service Specialist position. Customers loved me. When I think back, I think it's because of how I made my customers feel. I would always smile and greet people politely, and I would go above and beyond in everything I did.

I love to connect with people and show a genuine interest in wanting to know how they were that day, and how I could support them. These interactions improved my interpersonal skills as I was yarning and connecting with people. The skills in the early years of my career have helped me so much.

From St George Bank, I went to work with the Department of Community Services, where I worked with vulnerable families as a Brighter Futures Case Worker. Again, my skills in previous roles were very helpful in this position, as I was dealing with extremely complex situations. What I soon realised was that I had a passion for helping people and I wanted to use my experience to make a difference for others.

I went on to study to become a primary school teacher. I loved every minute of my career in education, where I worked in a few different jobs over 15 years. My love for education has provided me with a sense of passion and purpose and I feel I have made a difference to countless students and educators. I excelled in my role and went on to lead the Aboriginal Education Team and support the improvement journey of hundreds of schools. I am proud of my achievements that have led me to where I am now as the director of my own company. This is my next chapter of 'imagining the what if' and I'm sure I'll have a few stories to tell about my experience and all the lessons I'll learn along the way.

Tyrell

I've been lucky enough to work in different jobs, and in every job, I learnt something new. I was meant to do those jobs at that time in my life.

My first job was at Maccas. I didn't love it but I learnt about turning up on time, teamwork and working in a fast-paced environment. I enjoyed the money I made and the independence I felt making my own cash and spending it on whatever I wanted.

I've worked as a labourer for Sydney Trains. I made a lot of money working long hours and working away from home. I learnt a few things and realised I didn't like that type of work. I even worked as a bartender to test out that type of work environment. Again, I didn't love it, but it gave me experience and a sense of fulfilment as I got to try different things out and discovered what I didn't like.

The most rewarding, and longest, job I've held was working as a School Learning Support Officer with the Department of Education. I worked in a few different settings and enjoyed my time working with young people.

We never know unless we try so it's important to start somewhere. You may not land your dream job right away. You can't be too picky in your first few jobs as you need to build up your experience. As you gain skills and experience in one job, you can apply for other jobs that interest you.

Once you get a job, it's important that you develop a good work ethic by showing up on time and doing what's expected of you.

There is an abundance of jobs out there and the right job and career is waiting for you.

Have you taken some time to think about what you want to do?

You could go to uni and study business, law or education. You could go to TAFE or do a trade. You could be an electrician, a carpenter, a plumber, then you can start your own business.

You could be an entrepreneur, where you don't work for anyone. There is so much advice out there.

In fact, I think there's so much that sometimes it all just begins to sound like noise.

I am one of those people who cannot stay somewhere I don't want to be.

Obviously, everyone must put up with certain situations here and there as we need to start somewhere. I take this situation very personally, because it involves my time. If I stay somewhere I don't want to be, I feel like, day by day, my life is being spent carelessly, as if I'm throwing it down the drain.

It's hard to figure out what you want to do, especially if you don't know what kind of person you are.

It's important to try and figure out what you value.

For me, as I self-reflect, I realise that I value doing something that I think will be meaningful.

I value helping people.

I like to think of myself as an empathetic person.

I don't like the idea of other people suffering when they don't have to.

I like the idea that people have a sense of fulfillment in their lives.

The central focus of my values seems to be making the lives of other people better but not being a doormat. I value respect. I value progress. I value enjoying life.

As you get older, and your mind continues to grow, you'll learn more about yourself.

You'll also come to understand the value of knowing and listening to yourself.

You will become a master of yourself and know when it's worth persevering and when to pull the plug on something.

When thinking about your career choice it's important to think about the difference you want to make and all you hope to achieve. Your work does not have to be separate to your values, passions and interests. You can have it all and find a job that allows you to focus on your interests. When deciding on your ideal career it's important to think about the way you like to work.

Are you someone who prefers to work alone?

Do other people annoy you? Would rather work independently on project-based work or even run an online business?

Do you like being around people and working as part of a team?

Take time to think about your personality and how you like to interact with others.

There are many jobs out there that can give you the freedom of flexibility to focus on your personality and the values that you hold and the way you like to work.

When you think about your ideal job, it's important to do some research to find out what would be required for that job. It's important to think about the type of study and things you would need to do to get there.

For example, if you want to be a doctor, not only will you have to have a love for science and the human body, as well a genuine interest in taking care of people, but you'll also have to study things like maths.

The same goes for jobs in customer service. You must enjoy talking to people and problem solving, as well as dealing with challenging situations and customers. Many people love working with people and dealing with customers in a fast-paced environment. There are always new challenges and situations to face each day.

Learn – learn – learn!

Read inspirational books, listen to podcasts, or watch YouTube clips of people talking about their profession.

You may want to dabble in a few different things. You might have a passion project on the side and a business that allows you to do the things that you love.

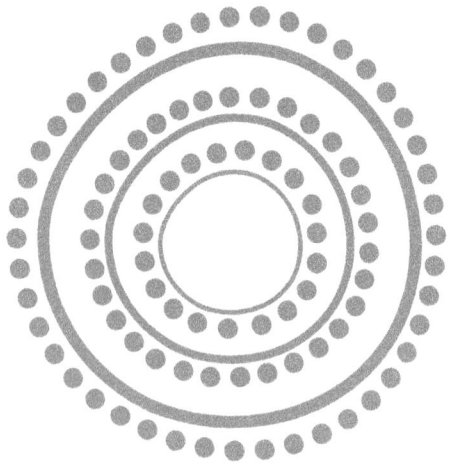

End of Chapter Reflection

Reflect on your interests, passions, and hobbies. What activities do you enjoy the most and could see yourself doing as a career?

- Think about your strengths and skills.
- What are you naturally good at?
- What subjects do you excel in at school?
- Explore different career options and research what each requires from you and what your responsibilities will be.
- Look into the education or training required, job responsibilities, and potential salary.
- Think about the impact you want to make in the world.
- What causes or issues are important to you?
- How can you align your career with making a difference?
- Seek advice from professionals in fields that interest you.
- Reach out to mentors, family, friends, or career counsellors who can provide insights and guidance.

- Consider your lifestyle preferences. Do you prefer a flexible schedule, working with a team, or working independently? Think about what kind of work environment and lifestyle would suit you best.
- Take advantage of opportunities for career exploration, such as internships, job shadowing or volunteering. These experiences can help you gain practical insights into different careers.
- Set short-term and long-term goals related to your career aspirations. Break them down into actionable steps and create a plan to work towards them.
- Embrace continuous learning and personal growth. Be open to acquiring new skills, expanding your knowledge, and adapting to changes in the industry.
- Don't be afraid to dream big and be ambitious in your career aspirations. Believe in yourself and your abilities and pursue a path that truly excites and motivates you.

"A person who never made a mistake, never tried anything new."
— C.S. Lewis

Chapter Three

BREAKING CYCLES AND EMBRACING EDUCATION

You can't be what you can't see is a term that is often used.

Sometimes, you need to see yourself in others to imagine yourself achieving those same goals.

This can make it hard for young people to see a bright future for themselves, especially if they don't see anyone around them achieving their dreams.

It's important to remember that if these cycles and 'lack of' appear in your world, you must remember that they don't have to continue.

You have the power to break that cycle and make a positive change.

You can be the change you wish to see.

Believe in yourself and work towards your dreams, even if it feels like they're out of reach.

We share this chapter to inspire you and show you that it's possible to create a better future for yourself and your community.

Being the first to break cycles in our families and communities can be tough.

Intergenerational trauma is passed on from generation to generation and is a heavy burden that affects many cultures.

Alongside this trauma, the lack of hope, dreams and aspirations becomes a common theme as well.

Sometimes, when we don't see role models within our own families or communities, we believe that our dreams are out of reach and unattainable.

We share our story for those who are striving to break free from the cycle and make positive changes in their lives.

We share our story to help you believe in yourself and your ability to pursue your dreams and goals.

Even if your upbringing, past choices, or lack of support make you doubt your capabilities, we urge you to take a moment to imagine the possibilities.

What if you could be the first in your family to succeed?

What if you could prove the doubters wrong and achieve your goals?

Once you get the taste of achievement, you may want more and want to keep pushing yourself to reach even greater dreams and goals.

If you've found yourself in a negative cycle, not sticking to your goals or heading down the wrong path, that cycle doesn't have to continue.

You have the power to break through any barriers that come your way and find solutions to the challenges you may face.

You've got this!

Think about the impact your success could have on the young people in your family or community.

Imagine how empowering it would be for them to witness your journey and realise that they too can achieve their goals.

You can be the person that inspires them to believe in themselves.

To make a positive change, the first step is to believe in your own worthiness and open your mind to the possibilities that await.

Through love, kindness, and compassion, each of us can contribute to creating a better world.

A world where all young people understand their potential to achieve anything they set their minds to.

Breaking the cycle involves facing our fears head-on.

Fear has a way of holding us back and, at times, causes us anxiety.

What if you could be the first to break free from the cycle that negatively impacts communities and pave the way for a purposeful and fulfilling life?

Kylie

I know what it's like to be trapped in a cycle of sadness and fear. It wasn't a path I consciously chose, but one that seemed to unfold naturally.

Sadly, I wasn't alone in this struggle.

At 17, I had a close brush with death that changed my life forever. The doctor couldn't explain how I survived, but I knew it was a miracle. My heart condition made my heart beat erratically and put my life at risk. My doctor doesn't know how I survived the dangerous rhythms he was seeing. All I remember is blacking out time after time, and thankfully, I survived, and I'm here to tell these yarns.

Back in my teenage years, my friends and I used to find entertainment in drinking. We'd go into a local pub where they sold us cheap alcohol with no labels. It was all fun and games until we ended up vomiting or passing out from excessive drinking. Little did I know that these reckless nights would lead me down a dangerous path.

After one particularly awful episode of alcohol poisoning, I found myself in the hospital, diagnosed with Long QT syndrome. I was frail and sick. It was a wake-up call. I was surrounded by elderly patients in the coronary care ward. Whenever my mum visited, I could see the fear in her eyes.

I felt miserable and weak, struggling just to keep my eyes open.

My excessive drinking was triggering my underlying heart condition. Thankfully, I received a diagnosis, unlike many others who suffer sudden deaths without warning signs. I was put on medication and regularly monitored by an incredible cardiologist, Dr Kuchar.

He had treated my mum years ago, alongside the famous Dr Victor Chang. It's thanks to this amazing doctor that I'm still here today. Sadly, Dr Kuchar passed away last year. He was a wonderful man who touched my heart – literally.

When I was 23, my cardiologist became concerned about my heart as I was showing a few issues. That's when he suggested I get my ICD, the electrical device inside my chest with the wires screwed into my heart, ready to zap my heart if needed. I've had the procedure three times now, and I jokingly refer to myself as a bionic woman, an unstoppable force because I'm battery powered lol.

Of course, it's no laughing matter and actually quite serious. Each and every day I express *gratitude for my strong, beating heart and my little friend inside me, ready to help if needed.*

My journey has taught me to appreciate life and to treasure each heartbeat as a gift. Now I dream big and imagine my life and the future I desire.

Despite the challenges, I keep going with hope and determination.

I share this story as it's the cycle of drinking and negative behaviour that I needed to break, and I did.

You can break cycles too.

Have a think about cycles or negative choices that impact those around you.

I would drink because that's what everyone else did. I thought it was normal. I realise now that there were other ways to find joy and numb some of the sadness I was feeling.

If I could go back in time, I would tell myself that everything was going to be okay. To keep smiling, to be kind to others, and particularly, be kind to myself. I would tell myself that I was smart and deadly and that I didn't need to be like everyone else. I just needed to be me!

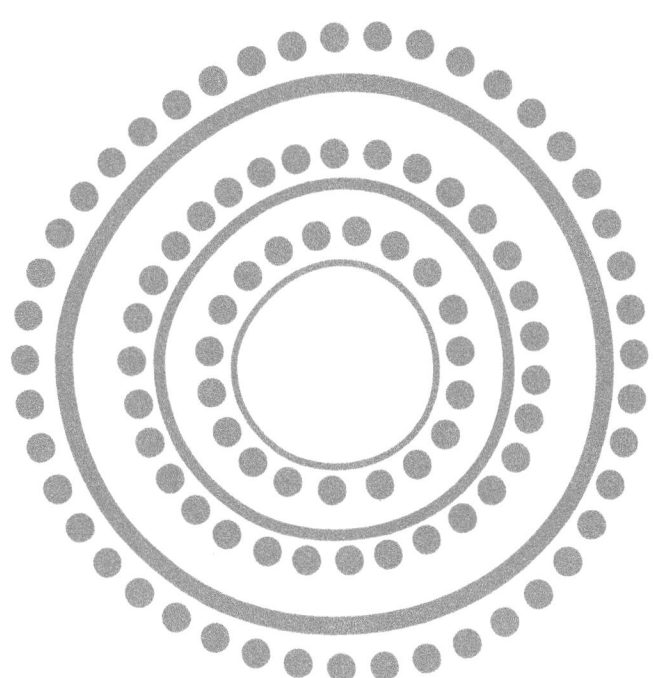

> "You are never too old to set another goal or to dream a new dream."
>
> – C.S. Lewis

That Teacher Who Made a Difference

At a very important time in my life, a teacher did something that changed my life and opened my mind to a world of possibilities. My teacher, Ms Burgess, planted the seed and believed in me and my ability.

She made me feel smart and capable of achieving. She said that she couldn't wait to see me in her Aboriginal Studies class the following year. This was massive as I was just about to drop out. I was in Year 10 with a very low attendance rate. I was heading down a very sad and negative path.

I remember how she made me feel and I started to think, "What if she's right?"

I wasn't planning to be in her class the following year as I didn't feel smart enough; however, I wanted to be the first person in my family to complete the HSC. I did achieve my HSC and as you've read, much, much more, thanks to my education and a kind teacher doing a few little things that made a difference for me. Around this time, my school also supported me with a work experience placement which also changed things for me.

All of a sudden, my path was becoming clearer, and I could see myself a few steps ahead kicking goals, smashing thorough barriers and breaking cycles.

My lesson here and message for you is to take those brave steps, as you never know unless you try. Trying is better than not even giving yourself a chance.

I'm now fortunate enough to work alongside my former teacher, as a co-author of my second book, and as President and Vice President of the Aboriginal Studies Association.

Dr Cathie Burgess is an amazing woman who has done so much for Aboriginal Education throughout her career, and I'm fortunate to continue to learn from her, and these days, teach her a few things too.

Some of the things I teach her are pretty basic. I created a QR code for an evaluation for one of our masterclasses recently. She thought I was *so smart and deadly, thinking I was some Tech Wizz for figuring that out, lol. I then showed her that you simply paste the link into a website and it generates it for you... haha. I felt deadly for teaching her something.*

I believe education is the driver of change and breaking the cycle.

We need to overcome any barriers that might be getting in the way.

Let's help and encourage each other to do better and be better.

I don't know how I did it, but I managed to break through.

We need to step outside our comfort zone and take those positive first steps if we want a better future for ourselves and our families.

What can you do to break the cycle?

I continue to work hard to be the best version of myself. I don't just do this for myself, I do it to inspire and motivate others as well.

I created a program called Dream Big which I designed to engage, inspire and motivate students about the importance of education and the power of goal setting. Tyrell and I now go into lots of schools to run the program and have motivational talks with students.

Throughout the program, students create vision boards and engage in journal writing. The purpose of vision boards is for students to display their dreams and goals creatively. They use their journals to set goals, both short-term and long-term, and are provided with prompts and strategies to break down their goals into simple and achievable steps.

In this program, I share my story of growing up in Waterloo and some of the struggles I faced. The message is of hope and resilience along with the strategies that I learnt to pick myself up and to dream big.

I encourage students to try to break the cycle and to try to inspire them to believe that their circumstances don't have to dictate their future.

My message to them is the message I hope you hear too!

Believe in yourself.

Dream big!

Go to school.

Ask for help when needed.

Be kind.

Express gratitude.

There is something powerful about the beauty of story sharing and vulnerability. It touches people's hearts and often gives hope to others.

Story sharing, honesty and vulnerability can really impact and make a difference to those around us.

Remember, we all have a story.

Your story matters.

You are the author of your story.

There are many people just like you who are out there dreaming big and working on creating the life of their dreams.

You are not alone.

Don't be shame!

See a few reflections from some of the students I've worked with below. They make me proud and I share because I want you to know there are many others out there breaking cycles and working towards goals just like you.

"Hey Kylie, thank you so much for coming and sharing your story. You were so positive. You really did inspire me. I am going to do better and try harder. You made me feel that I am capable of achieving anything. Thank you!"

"I will be kinder to myself and stop worrying about what other people think. I realise that I have not been true to myself or put myself first. I am a stronger and different person now – thank you."

"I have always been seen as funny and tough. Always there to stick up for anyone and help whoever needed help. I now feel that I have not been there for myself and that I need to take care of me before I can help and be there for others. I'm going to look after myself, work towards achieving my goals and also make an effort to mend some important relationships with people I care about."

"After participating in this program and taking the time to think about my dreams and goals, I realise just how precious life is. I'm going to dream bigger and work harder."

When setting your goals or thinking about your future, I encourage you to think about your own family, community, or the things that you're passionate about that can help bring out the motivation you need.

For me, my purpose has stemmed from my own experiences and challenges.

For example, I went on to study to be a teacher, and eventually, was brave enough to share my story because of the difference a teacher made in my life.

They were many people who have believed in me and saw my potential. It's for this reason that I feel it's important that I give back and do the same for others.

I used this passion to keep me motivated when I embarked on a journey of studying full-time and working full-time whilst raising my two young children.

There were many times I wanted to give up, but I kept thinking that I needed to do this and that I wanted to do this because they were many young people who needed me.

Are there areas in your family of community that you feel you could help with?

You could have a passion for dance and see that there are no dance groups in your area.

You could be from a remote community where health issues are a problem that needs solving, or you may feel that your people or community and not being treated fairly.

These could be the passion points that steer you into building a life and career based on your values and desires to make a difference and live out your dream.

Other examples could be things like social justice, lack of services or businesses in the areas of beauty, hospitality, resources, clothing, design, land management... the possibilities are endless.

I dedicate my life and career to education by empowering more educators to understand our history and our rich and beautiful culture that is there for all to learn about.

I love sharing my knowledge and experience with educators in order to help them to build empathy and understanding.

Tyrell

My mum believes that education is the key to a successful life, and I think there is truth in that. Education is where we learn how to interpret the world. In English, you learn vocabulary and *creative writing; you learn comprehension and new ways of seeing the world around you.*

Mathematics teaches you that there is an answer to every problem and that you must work it out.

Without my education, I wouldn't be able to think the way I do today.

As you can see from some of the stories I've shared throughout the book, you learn a lot more than the curriculum when you pay attention at school. I was lucky enough to get an education at a great school. I finished year 12 and got my HSC. There were times when things were hard, but I reached out to the teachers, and they supported me through my journey. Many teachers actually want you to succeed. It's their job to do what they can to support you, and it's your job to put in the work.

I went to Christian Brothers High School in Lewisham. Many of the staff at my school provided me with so much support – everything from believing in me to helping me structure a sentence. I had my Aboriginal Education Officer,

Kaleb Taylor, my support teacher, Mrs Marea Soulos, home room teacher, Mr Leigh Magri, and the Assistant Principal of my school house, Mr Peter Roumie. All of these people and many others were on my team, backing me to do my best and reach my potential.

When you really want something and are committed to pursuing a goal, teachers and support staff naturally want to help you. If you are ever struggling with something, whether it's workload or your grades, it could be anything, don't be scared to reach out and ask for help. There are so many great programs that schools run to support students, and there are so many great teachers who are eager to support and see you be the best you can be.

We encourage you to reflect on this chapter and look at areas in your life or community where you can put a stop to negative patterns and help break the cycle.

There is always a new day and opportunity to start fresh. A chance to hit the reset button and take those first positive steps in the right direction as you never know where they'll lead.

As we reflect on our experiences as teens and the journey we've been on, we can't help but be thankful for where we ended up.

We attribute so much of our success to the power of education. Teachers and staff at school believed in us, which opened our minds to the power of dreams and exploring the 'what if'.

All the lessons have allowed us to break the cycle and choose our path.

What if you took that leap of faith and had a go?

What if you stopped doing something negative and replaced it with something positive?

We believe in you!

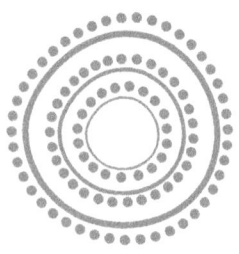

"You don't have to be great to start, but you have to start to be great."

– Zig Ziglar

PART B

QUICK READS TO INSPIRE AND MOTIVATE

> *"Education is the passport to the future, for tomorrow belongs to those who prepare for it today."*
> *– Malcolm X*

Not a reader? That's okay, here you'll find bits and pieces of info and inspo that just may inspire you to take action and lead you from where you are to where you want to be.

You could use this section as part of your morning routine, especially if you are working towards changing your daily habits. Completing a small goal in the morning, such as reading, can be your first win and put you in a good headspace for the rest of the day.

You can flick to any page and read a little inspiration anytime to help start your day right. Know that any day is a good time to start. You don't have to wait until Monday or the start of a new month or new year. Know that you can start NOW!

> "You are braver than you believe,
> stronger than you seem
> and smarter than you think."
> – A.A. Milne

Dreaming Big Will NOT Work Without Taking Action

We can dream away as much as we like, however, we also need to take the steps to move towards that dream. Dreaming is the first step though. Everything starts with a thought. Allow yourself to put lots of energy into this first step. Close your eyes and dream away. See yourself living your dream, fast forward to the end of your dream and see yourself celebrating as if it's already yours. Get excited and celebrate the fact that you made it. It could be celebrating the end of exams, getting that job, getting into uni, making that sporting team, saving money... the list goes on. Step one of dreaming big is dreaming, so allow yourself to do exactly that. However, dreams don't come true without putting in the work too. We need to get up, show up and go get it.

Mornings are great times for dreaming, so try waking up a half hour earlier and allocate yourself some dreaming time. See below a few steps that can help you get started.

- Name your dream. Write it down, journal about it or create a vision board to help keep your dream alive.
- See it in your mind (dream away).
- See it as already yours.

- ◎ Celebrate and be proud of your achievement.
- ◎ Make a plan.
- ◎ Step it out.
- ◎ Figure out who can help you.
- ◎ Commit to your plan.
- ◎ Schedule in time to work towards your dream.
- ◎ Prepare for possible disruptions. The better we plan, the better we'll handle situations if and when they arise.
- ◎ Surround yourself with people you admire. If you like a particular person for their strengths or courage, or how they respectfully interact with others, rub shoulders with them and find opportunities to interact with and learn from them.

> **"Thoughts become things."**
> *– Bob Proctor*

Education Changes Lives

Education is our passport to freedom. We need the essential skills that education provides. Education teaches us perspective and critical thinking. We learn to read, write, and use logic in many subjects, including mathematics, science, geography.

Importantly, education gives us the skills to navigate life. The best thing about education is that it can never be taken from you. Once you learn specific skills, they're yours. Keep them in your invisible backpack and pull them out when needed.

Remember, you don't have to be the smartest. You don't have to be the wisest. Use education to give you two things we all need, and two things you deserve – freedom and choice.

I embrace education and use the skills to empower me to live out my dreams and goals. I'm grateful to live in a country where I have access to a quality education.

Finding Balance Between School, Home and Social Activities

We know your teens are busy times. There is so much you need to do – go to school, do your homework, do your assignments, clean your room, help out around the house, get to sport, stay connected with friends, and possibly care for family members, siblings, pets, etc...

It's important that you try to find a healthy balance between all of these activities. It's also important to know how to transition from one activity to the next. Many adults practice these transition points from work to home. For example, they use the drive on the way home from work to centre themselves before stepping in the door at home so they can be fully present when they are home with their families, rather than carrying the burdens and stories and busyness of work into the home environment.

You need to find your little transition points. If you're leaving school for the day, take a few minutes to prepare your mind for your next activity.

Think about what's next. If you're heading to sports, tutoring or to a friend's house, take a few moments to think ahead and visualise how you are going to show up in that situation.

How do you want to enter? Do you want to be smiling? What sort of energy do you want to bring? What type of conversations do you want to have? You don't have to overthink it and put too much time into it, but it can be helpful to take a few moments to think about the transition points and how you want your activities to play out.

When moving on to your next activity, possibly arriving home – think about what will happen when you arrive. Will it be dinner time? Do you need to take out the rubbish, do your chores or have a difficult conversation with a parent or carer? Take a few moments to think ahead and plan for how you want to show up in all of those moments.

Don't just stumble from one activity to the next, waiting to see how things go. Plan ahead, be in control, and choose how you want to be seen and behave in each situation in your life.

> *I choose my thoughts wisely. I choose my words wisely. I choose my actions wisely. I create my path through my beliefs, and the actions that I take.*

Strengthening Your Resilience

Resilience is a word that gets used a lot. It means the ability to bounce back from a disruption, challenge or significant life event.

Experiencing tough times can be hard, and everyone will demonstrate their resilience differently.

Having strategies to help cope with challenging times is essential.

There is no right or wrong way to cope or react to significant life events. Some can tap into and implement their coping mechanisms easily, while others may struggle to move forward.

Think about the coping mechanisms that work for you when times get tough and the supportive people you can call on if and when needed. Know they'll be there, ready to use if and whenever you need them.

You know you best, so think about what works for you.

> **"The past can hurt, but from the way I see it, we can either run from it or learn from it."**
> *– The Lion King*

Fear of Failure

Once you find your resilience, there will always be fears that pop up, which often stop us from moving forward. Embarking on a new job, trying something different, or doing something unfamiliar to your friends, family and community can be daunting in case we fail. We pay so much attention to what others think and how they perceive us. At times, this stops us from moving forward with our dreams and goals. We need to take control of our lives and not allow others to choose our path. We decide where to for ourselves. Unfortunately, we see it far too often, where people want to tear each other down rather than build each other up. We encourage you to find your resilience, and if you can, help others find theirs too. Find your passion and don't let fear of failure get in the way.

> **"Failure is the opportunity to begin again more intelligently."**
> – Henry Ford

Be Proud of Your Culture

We are proud of our rich and beautiful culture. Aboriginal people were the first engineers and the first scientists. Community, caring for Country, and identity are essential things that ensure our survival for generations. We are proud of who we are and do our best to make a difference for our people.

If you call Australia home, we think you should learn about Aboriginal histories and cultures. Ask questions, read books, show respect for Country and be part of your local community. Share parts of your own culture too. Culture makes us who we are. Some may think they don't have a culture. However, once you learn about its true meaning, we're sure you'll recognise the culture that surrounds you.

Think about what is special and unique about your culture. It could be the food, celebrations, connections, traditions or values. Embrace it and be proud of who you are.

Be proud of your culture.
Your culture makes you YOU!

Study Routines

Study routines are essential. Like everything, they always seem tricky at the beginning, but once you get into a routine, you can try to make it a habit. The more you practice these habits, the less time and energy you'll need to make them happen.

Below are a few points to consider that may help you.

Firstly, ensure you minimise distractions and let people know when you study. Tell your friends and family your study schedule, and don't let anything interrupt it. Sticking to these habits can minimise the stress and anxiety that build up when you fall behind.

Take yourself away from things or places that might cause you to be distracted. If you have pets that are annoying and distracting, make sure you're away from them as well. Choose somewhere you feel relaxed and away from responsibilities and people who may interrupt you.

Be sure to allow yourself time to take a breather. Be sure to schedule breaks to get some fresh air. Try study sessions for 40 to 50 minutes, then schedule a 10-minute break and then try another timed session. Set yourself a timer and know that you can't touch your phone or do anything else until that timer goes off.

By putting in some effort and creating study routines, you may find yourself more in control and have reduced stress levels around studying and assignments.

If you have a group of friends or individuals you can be productive with, team up and set some study goals together. Make it a fun game and schedule your study times, then relaxation times. Before you start, write down a couple of goals you hope to achieve that day and smash them out.

> **"You can have, do or be anything you want."**
> – Dr Joe Vatale

Procrastination Hacks

If you find you're often procrastinating, which means that you are delaying or postponing the things that need to get done, don't worry, you're not alone.

There are many skills and techniques you can learn to implement into your daily routine to smash through procrastination.

A few simple things could include writing down up to three tasks you want to achieve. Set yourself a timer on your phone and start it. As you achieve the first goal, cross it off. By crossing them off as you go, you're creating a sense of achievement. We're human and we love achieving things.

Before you even start, think about how to reward yourself once you achieve your goals.

It could be that you are going to allow yourself to have a treat, ring a friend who you know will bring you joy, or you'll go and physically see someone or do something. Think of a meaningful reward, and only allow yourself to get that reward once you have achieved your goal.

Planning is essential. As is thinking about the blockers and the things that might get in the way and sabotage your success. Allow your mind to wander briefly to the things that may interrupt you. It could be notifications on your phone, someone calling you, a dog, a parent, or a family member needing your support. Think of how you can sort these things before they become an issue and interfere with your study goals that day.

> **"Procrastination makes easy things hard and hard things harder."**
> *– Mason Cooley*

Challenge Negative Thoughts

Our minds can often play tricks on us. Negative thoughts may creep in and show up without warning and try to convince us to make decisions we don't want to make. For example, they may have you think that you can't clean your room because you're too tired or you don't have the energy to do it.

They may have you think that you can't exercise because you didn't sleep well or that you shouldn't apply for that job because you won't get it anyway.

Try to get moving and take action before you start to believe those thoughts.

When negative thoughts creep in, challenge them. Ask yourself if they're based on facts or assumptions. Our minds can magnify our doubts, making them seem more significant than they really are. So, when you notice a negative thought creep in, try your best to challenge it and replace it with healthier and more positive thoughts where you can.

> "You are enough just as you are."
> – Meghan Markle

Smashing Through Self-Doubt

When life throws us a challenge, self-doubt often sets in; however, sometimes, it's where a lot of people get stuck. Becoming stuck doesn't allow us to move forward with our dreams.

Strengthen your belief in yourself and work through the doubt. Use your positive self-talk or reach out to someone and ask them for advice. You probably know what they'll say, however, when self-doubt kicks in, we all need a little reassurance and pep talk to strengthen our belief in our abilities.

> *I take on challenges with courage and determination.*

Never Suffer in Silence

Don't ever be ashamed to reach out for help. Never suffer in silence. There is always someone or something that can help. The campaign *'It's okay not to be okay'* unpacks the stigma around mental health and opens the door for a conversation. We all know someone who struggles with mental health and at times, we all may suffer. We can all do our part to build a community that supports each other through life's challenges. It's important that we all have a special someone we can call on when times get tough.

Contact the Kids Help Line on 1800 551 800, reach out to Beyond Blue, or speak to a teacher or trusted adult for help and support.

> "Everything will be okay in the end.
> If it's not okay, it's not the end."
> – John Lennon

First Impressions Count

Let's talk about something that can truly shape your interactions and relationships – first impressions.

Did you know that it's been said that people often form judgements about you within the first three seconds of meeting you? It's crazy to think this is so, however when we think about it, we guess it sounds right. With this knowledge, it's important to make a positive impact from the very start.

Imagine walking into a room or meeting someone new. How you present yourself during those initial moments can leave a lasting impression.

It's important to make connections and make others feel important and valued. Relationships are important. A genuine smile and a focused interest in what the other person has to say can create a strong foundation for a meaningful connection.

In today's fast-paced world, taking the time to truly listen to someone can make all the difference. Often, we're so eager to respond that we miss out on the opportunity to understand their perspective fully. This can send the message that we're not entirely engaged in the conversation. So, next time you're meeting someone, challenge yourself to actively listen and show genuine interest.

Remember, the first impression you create sets the tone for how others perceive you.

Whether you're in a job interview, meeting a potential friend, or interacting with someone you admire, those first few seconds count.

*I make a positive
impact wherever I go.*

The Good and The Bad of Socials

Yep, you knew we were going there. How can we write a motivational book for teens without talking about the elephant in the room and the damage it does to young people?

As much as we love social media, as it's a big part of our life and society, we can't let it ruin us. We must protect ourselves from the negatives associated with it.

We all know there is so much good and bad when it comes to social media. Here, we're going to share a few little yarns about the pros and cons in hope to help you find a nice balance that suits you.

Social media is an amazing platform to connect and feel close to others. It allows us to share our life and world with others where we can connect and feel valued and acknowledged.

It can also cause many issues in our lives as we all know the negative impacts. Bullying and all the anxiety caused around 'keyboard warriors' and people saying nasty things are just some of the negative impacts.

How can you use social for good and protect yourself from the negatives?

> *I make smart choices and use my time and experience online for good.*

Be Mindful of What You Share Online

Be mindful of the personal information you share online. You don't always have to overshare. Save some of your news and updates for real life and those closest to you who get to see the 'real you'. You may want to check out your privacy settings to be mindful of who can see what you share. There are so many amazing things about social media. Most of us use it and enjoy all it has to offer, however just because you see others sharing every little thing about their life, it doesn't mean that you have to. You can pick and choose the aspects which you want others to see about you, your life and who you are. Don't feel like you have to follow the crowd and do what everyone else is doing online. Be unique and be you.

Don't get caught up in sending and receiving inappropriate images. There are so many inappropriate things that happen these days with phones, texting, sexting, and sending all sorts of crazy and disgusting things. Don't get yourself into trouble or in an unsafe situation by sending or even being on the receiving end of some of this stuff. If someone sends you something you don't like or shouldn't be receiving, block, report and delete. Don't engage with it.

Try and take some time to think before you post. Remember that once you share something it's really difficult to take it down or to erase it. As you know, people take screenshots and can sometimes manipulate what you say.

Be sensible and protect yourself from something you may regret.

Think about how you want to be seen on social media. Some people have an incredibly positive presence and share their incredible ideas and stories that inspire and motivate others.

Others use it as a really negative space. Often fuelled by jealousy, anger and criticism, there are people who use social media poorly to troll and to gain power. They feel they can belittle others through the words they share behind their computer or devices.

I make sensible choices.

Don't Engage in the Negative Stuff

Avoid engaging in cyberbullying and negativity. Remember that there are real people behind the profiles, and your words can have a significant impact. Everyone has something going on in their lives so be mindful of your words and actions. Engaging in gossip, drama and negative stuff is such an energy zapper. Choose where you give your precious energy and put it to good use.

You should always be kind and respectful. Treat others with kindness. Think about how you like to be treated and be that person. If you're not seeing your friends or those you engage with be kind and demonstrate values of positivity and motivation, be sure you lead by example.

> **"In a world where you can be anything, be kind."**
> *– Jennifer Dukes Lee*

Manage Your Time Wisely

Manage your time wisely and don't give socials your life. Social media can be addictive and we all give it too much of our valuable time. Try setting some boundaries and allocate times for using social media. Perhaps you could try turning off the notifications, so they don't buzz or show up with the little symbols to let you know if somebody has liked or commented on something.

Start to monitor how much time you spend online so you can become aware. Not everyone has an issue with social media but what we do know is that it's a big part of life, and there are so many people experiencing social fatigue, and even mental health problems, from the anxiety social media creates.

Try setting up a weekly schedule and even use the calendar in your phone to allocate times for social media, particularly when you're trying to study and get through assignments and school-related tasks.

My time is valuable.

Build a Positive Online Presence

Is there an opportunity for you to build a positive presence on social media? Can you brainstorm a little passion project that you could build a positive online presence for? Brainstorm a few ideas and map out a bit of plan for how you want to be seen online.

Enjoy your time on social media if that's what you love. Know that it is an incredible tool for creativity, friendships and inspiration. Don't let it take control and consume too much of your time. If it is starting to cause you stress or anxiety or if it is impacting on your other commitments, such as school, household chores or work commitments, please take some time to make some adjustments.

> "Every day is a great day to give love, spread joy and sparkle."
> – Sheri Fink

Road Safety and Driving With Friends

Let's delve into a topic that's crucial for your wellbeing – staying safe. Especially, when it comes to driving and various situations you might encounter.

As you gain independence and start spending more time with friends and exploring the world, it's essential to make informed choices that prioritise your safety.

When it comes to driving, remember that it's not just about getting from point A to point B; it's about doing so responsibly.

The first time you get behind the wheel can be exciting, but it's crucial to respect the power of a vehicle and understand the risks involved. Think about your actions on the road, and always prioritise the safety of yourself, your passengers, and those around you.

Choosing who you ride with is equally important. Your friends might have their licenses, but it doesn't mean every situation is safe. Trust your instincts and pay attention to how the driver behaves. If you notice distractions, excessive speed, or risky behaviour, don't hesitate to speak up and remove yourself from the situation if necessary. Your wellbeing should always come first.

Consider the statistics related to teen driving accidents.

The numbers can be eye-opening, reminding us all that being a responsible driver and passenger is paramount.

By knowing the risks and being aware of your surroundings, you can contribute to safer roads for everyone.

Beyond driving, remember that the choices you make in various situations can impact your safety as well.

Whether it's choosing where to hang out, who to spend time with, or how to react in certain scenarios, trust your instincts and prioritise your wellbeing.

In a world filled with opportunities and experiences, making smart and safe choices is key.

Your life's journey is a precious one, and it's up to you to protect it. Always prioritise your safety, whether you're on the road or navigating life's adventures.

My safety is my priority.

Recognise Your Strengths

Finding your strengths is an important part of your personal development, especially as you navigate your education, career choices and personal growth. It may sound a bit weird when you're asked to try to recognise your strengths. You may be wondering what that even means.

We all have unique qualities and talents that make us who we are.

Recognising your strengths is taking time the to reflect on the things you're good at or the things you enjoy. Focusing on these positive things can help boost your confidence help you feel better about yourself.

Take time to think about what makes you feel good.

What activities excite you?

Your interests can be a clue to your strengths. You don't have to know it all now, perhaps you'll take some time to think about this and start to notice your strengths.

> **"Life is interesting... in the end,
> some of your greatest pains,
> become your greatest strengths."**
> – Drew Barrymore

Set Small Goals

Setting achievable goals can help you build your confidence over time. When you accomplish these goals, no matter how small they might seem, you'll see that you can achieve what you set your mind to.

Think about what gets you out of bed in the morning. What can you be doing to make your day, your week, and your time more purposeful? What are a couple of little things that you can do to work towards?

Start small and allow yourself to feel what it feels like to achieve success. It could be as simple as getting out of bed by your first alarm or deciding to send a text message to someone you care about once a week.

Setting little goals and adding them to your notes on your phone, or in a diary, then working towards them each week can bring you an amazing sense of achievement. It's empowering to put a line through them or tick them off. Start working towards some of those small but important goals to help you be your best.

> "What you think you become.
> What you feel you attract.
> What you imagine you create."
> – *Buddha*

Either Win or Learn

This is the title of John Kavanagh's book about Conor McGregor, a MMA fighter, who does a lot of work on the power of his mind as well as his physical self to succeed.

Setbacks and failures are a natural part of life. Instead of letting failure reinforce your self-doubt, view it as an opportunity to learn and grow. Every setback brings a lesson that can make you stronger. Of course, you'll feel disappointed when things don't go your way – we all do – however, there will always be something we can learn from things that don't go our way and in fact, it can help build our strength and resilience.

> "Change your thoughts and
> you will change your world."
> – Norman Vincent Peale

Practice Self-Care

Treat yourself with the same kindness and understanding that you would offer to a friend.

Many people think self-care is about getting a mani, pedi or a massage. In fact, self-care is more than treating yourself to pamper days or gifting yourself things.

Check-in to ensure your body, mind and spirit are all aligned and taken care of. Self-care could mean taking time out for a massage, a long walk, or turning your phone off and watching a funny movie. Whatever self-care means to you and makes you feel good – do that.

Self-care involves looking after yourself, both inside and out. Make good hygiene a self-care priority too. Little things like wearing sunscreen daily and putting moisturiser on your skin can affect how you feel about yourself. Looking good can help us feel good. You know the basics, brush your teeth, shower often, and use deodorant.

Take care of your mind, your spirit and your body, and they will take care of you.

How do you take care of you?

Can you take better care of yourself?

I practice self-care. I prioritise my health and ensure that I always put myself first.

Nourish Your Body

While we're in good health, it's important to think of ways to sustain our health. Taking care of what we put in our body is extremely important. Many people don't get enough nutrients. Many of us are in a hurry and fuelling ourselves with fast food, that often have very little nutrients. There are certain things that we can all do to ensure we're getting enough.

It's important to ensure you get enough sleep and water to help us be our best. Taking a simple daily vitamin could be a great strategy too. These days, you can find them in jellies and lots of other forms. You may even want to try greens. You can even add them to a protein shake, so you're getting your protein and nutrients all in one.

Of course, we can't go past the good old-fashioned fresh fruit and vegetables. Think of a few ways in which you can nourish your body. Set up healthy routines to ensure you are getting enough of the things you need to be your best.

I enjoy nourishing my body with the nutrients it needs. I always try to give my body what it needs so I can be my best.

Seek Support When Needed

Don't hesitate to talk to someone you trust about your feelings. Friends, family members, teachers or counsellors can provide valuable perspectives and encouragement. If you don't feel comfortable starting a conversation, try sending a text, email or even writing a letter to express your feelings. Don't ever feel ashamed for reaching out for help or support. We all do it and it really is okay. Those that can support you often like helping and supporting too, so don't ever feel like you're a burden.

I'm not afraid to ask for help when I need it. There is no shame in asking for assistance.

Focus on Progress, Not Perfection

Instead of aiming for perfection, aim for progress. Remember that personal growth is a journey, and it's about becoming better over time, not about being flawless. Slowly, slowly, even if you're just 1% better each time. Sometimes you may take a few steps back, then go forward, and that's okay too. Keep going and never give up.

> **"Have the courage to be imperfect."**
> *– Alfred Fidler*

Avoid Comparing

Comparing yourself to others can spiral your thoughts into a never-ending pattern of self-doubt. Remember that everyone has a story and things they are dealing with. Social media and the things people share often only showcases a positive version of people's lives. Don't give others' lives too much energy and instead, focus on being the best you can be.

I am special and unique just the way I am. I love every part of me and I'm learning to accept who I am. I do not compare myself with others – I am me.

Mindfulness

There seems to be an abundance of things to be stressed or worried about. We live in a society where never-ending worries are brought to our attention each day, creating a powerful concoction of fear, anxiety, stress and overwhelm. Mindfulness is a word that gets used often and isn't about sitting on a meditation cushion chanting "Om". It is everything from paying attention to the flavours as you eat, to going for a walk and listening to the sounds around you.

Mindfulness and/or meditation can help us stay calm and relaxed. We suggest you give it a go. There are many mindfulness practices. Some may be meditation, journaling, colouring in, yoga, walking – there are many. You can even turn doing your chores into a mindfulness practice. Doing the dishes can be therapeutic if you want it to be. Anything from vacuuming to watering plants can be mindfulness. Decluttering is a great mindfulness practice too. It always seems like a massive chore before you get started but once you get going it can become a therapeutic exercise.

Our minds are always wandering off thinking about something else rather than the task at hand, which is to remain present. You can practice mindfulness to stay present and curb negative self-talk by replacing self-doubting thoughts with positive affirmations.

The stillness and slow breathing is comforting. Meditation, or quieting your mind, allows your thoughts to come and go. It gives us the opportunity to reflect and process the things we need to help be our best.

Meditation can bring a whole new level of clarity and purpose to your life.

Give it a go and see what it does for you.

You also can use this practice to remind yourself of your strengths and accomplishments.

Mindfulness means being in the present moment. Worrying about the past or future takes us away from what we truly can have an impact on – the here and now.

*I focus on the here
and now.*

Celebrate Your Achievements

Whenever you achieve something, no matter how small, take a moment to celebrate it. Recognising your accomplishments can help shift your focus away from doubts.

Remember, overcoming self-doubt is a process that takes time and effort. Be patient with yourself and believe in your ability to overcome challenges. You have the power within you to build confidence and embrace your unique qualities.

> "I'm a dreamer. I have to dream and reach for the stars, and if I miss then I grab a handful of clouds."
> – Mike Tyson

Morning Routine

Do you have a morning routine?

One that doesn't involve phones or unhealthy habits?

You might be wondering, "Why is having a morning routine even important?"

It can make a big difference in how you approach your day and how you feel overall.

Imagine starting your day with a sense of purpose and clarity, rather than hitting the snooze button a dozen times and rushing to get ready.

A morning routine helps you begin your day mindfully. Instead of immediately diving into emails, social media, or other distractions, you can dedicate time to focus on yourself and your wellbeing.

Starting your day right can have a huge impact on your productivity, mindset and anxiety levels… yep, we all suffer from those.

What is the very first thing that you do?

Do you reach for your phone and check social media or do you start scrolling and mindlessly worry about what everybody else is doing?

The first hour of the day should be our time.

It's so easy to get caught up in the stuff that everybody else is doing and things that are external from our own immediate self.

As hard as it is sometimes, it's important to try to dedicate time in the morning to focus on you and how you want your day to look.

You might not see this right now, but it is true. It's so important to invest time into you.

Here are tips to try to have a more productive day and create the life of your dreams.

Start by setting an alarm and getting straight up.

Don't overthink it. Just get up! Mel Robbins, author of 'The 5 Second Rule', says that there is science and research about the power of getting up within 5 seconds of waking.

If we hit the snooze button our brain starts to wind back down, and it takes about two hours to get going again.

If you get a chance, listen to her podcast or her book on Audible. Waking and getting ready in the morning can be hard, however, it's amazing when you think about how quickly you wake up if you put a little effort into it.

Once that alarm goes off jump up and head straight to the bathroom. Say to yourself, "Wake up, wake up, wake up!"

A consistent routine can boost your productivity. When you follow a set pattern, your brain gets the signal that it's time to get into gear. This can help you tackle tasks more efficiently throughout the day.

Starting the day in a chaotic rush can leave you feeling stressed.

A well-structured morning routine can help you begin your day in a calm and collected manner, reducing stress levels.

Including activities like meditation, journaling or exercise in your morning routine can positively impact your mental health. These activities can set a positive tone for your mindset throughout the day.

A morning routine is an opportunity to integrate healthy habits into your life. Whether it's drinking water, stretching or reading, these habits can gradually become a natural part of your daily life.

Having a routine brings structure to your day. Knowing what to expect in the morning can give you a sense of control and stability.

Accomplishing tasks in the morning, even small ones, can boost your confidence and give you a sense of achievement. This positive feeling can carry over into other aspects of your life.

*I enjoy starting my day right
by taking care of me first.*

Kylie's JEM Morning

There are many different morning routines you can create. I like to keep it simple and practice my JEM Morning.

Journal – Exercise – Meditate.

They're not always in that order – I try to do those three things even when I am time poor. If I only have two minutes to spend on each of them, I will simply spend two minutes on each – being a total of six minutes of my time. Let me tell you, even that six minutes can make a difference. If I am going to speak at a big conference or to an important meeting, spending six minutes on these things will put me in a really good headspace and allow me to be focused and intentional with how I want my day to look.

I use my Dream Big Journal or another beautiful journal. I write the date and I just start to express what I'm grateful for or even my plan for the day. It's like having a friend who is just there listen. It's really therapeutic and there is a lot of research and evidence to support how good it is for us.

> I start my day right. I plan how
> I want my day and week to look.
> I am intentional with my actions.

Life Skills

Life skills are important, especially as you get older. Not only do life skills allow us to develop independence and get ready for adult life, they also help us feel a sense of fulfilment and pride. Knowing how to do things for yourself is a wonderful skill to have.

Below you'll find a few of the basics. Don't worry, we're not going to bore you too much with this stuff, but it's important so hopefully you take something away if you're not yet testing out your independence.

Every day I am learning new skills. Skills that will empower me now and into the future.

Independent You

Mastering Laundry and Cooking

Do you know how to cook?

If not, it's good to start thinking about a few basic meals you can prepare for yourself and maybe even your friends and family. Takeaway is delicious, fast and easy, but it's expensive and we need to learn some basic cooking skills. Think about the foods that you most enjoy eating – burgers, curries, pasta etc.

You may have someone in your life that prepares these meals for you, however, it's important for you to learn the skills and how to prepare these foods and have a go making them. Watch and learn from someone, then ask them to prepare it alongside you before you independently have a go yourself.

There will be times in the future where you will live independently or not have this person there to show you the way, so take the opportunities while you can.

Think about what you like to eat for breakfast. Are you a cereal and toast person? Or do you love a bit of egg and smashed avo? Breakfast at a cafe is expensive, whereas if you learn to prepare these things at home, you will save so much money.

The great thing about where you are in life is that you have the internet and YouTube at your fingertips. You can literally type in the recipe that you're after and be shown step-by-step instructions.

Depending on your cultural background and the types of flavours you like, it's good to think about a few staples to have.

Think of three dishes you could create for dinner and have a go at making them. You can also have it for lunch the next day.

It's also a good idea to use timers when cooking. Look up things like how long you should boil pasta for and set a timer for it, as it's easy to get distracted and forget.

A good cook is a clean cook so try to be fast, efficient and tidy as you go.

Don't create a huge mess and then leave it till the end and start the whole clean-up process.

Simply Google what you're after and it'll take you to website such as taste.com.au where all of your ingredients are outlined with the step-by-step instructions.

It's also important to know how to wash and dry your own clothes. Even if you have the luxury of someone doing it for you, try your best to learn these basic skills. Every washing machine is different – you should know what setting to have it on, where to put the detergent and the fabric softener, and basic things like sorting colours and remembering to check pockets for tissues or paper – all those basic things will make a difference for you.

Many people struggle to live independently because the basic skills outlined here had not been practised in their younger years. It's important to know what clothes shouldn't go in the dryer, as the dryer can shrink your clothing. Read the label to see what the recommendation is. Happy washing and enjoy the feeling of independence.

I enjoy being independent and learning new things. I have hands to do things for myself and a brain to figure things out.

Managing Money and Saving

Everyone should know how to manage money.

You could win the Lotto tomorrow and quickly lose it all if you don't have good financial literacy skills. These skills are crucial to start to learn and embed in your life as early as possible.

Even if you don't have much money, it's good to be thrifty and to know how to spend and save wisely.

Now is also a good time to make sure you have a bank account, so if you don't have one already, this could be something you put on your to-do list. You'll need identification to open one, so make sure you have the appropriate ID and if you're under 18, you'll usually need a parent or guardian to sign your paperwork.

Have two accounts if possible. Most banks these days allow you to have student accounts with zero fees so be sure to make sure you don't have an account that has unnecessary fees attached.

Once you have a bank account, create a budget. Think about all the things you need to spend your money on. You can use the notes in your phone. Your list could look like:

- Phone credit or bill
- Eating out
- Gym membership

No matter how small your savings may be, we encourage you to start saving now.

Think about some of the things that you would like to save for. It could be a new mobile phone, new shoes, a new hair straightener, makeup, clothing, a holiday or even saving to buy yourself a car or a house in the future. There is beauty in saving and watching your bank account grow.

Start developing healthy financial literacy now, and it will serve you well into the future. Generational wealth is something we all should be thinking about. Think about the finances and lifestyle you desire now and start working towards achieving what you want. You can have anything your heart desires, so go for it and make your dreams a reality.

*When money flows into my life,
I manage it well by spending wisely.
I save for the things I desire. I enjoy creating wealth for my future.*

Navigating the Ups and Downs of Emotions

Teenage years are tough when it comes to dealing with the ups and downs of emotions. Your body is growing and changing, as are your hormones and emotions. Each chapter in life comes with its own challenges.

It's important to understand that sometimes being on an emotional roller coaster is very normal.

Everyone will feel the various emotions that make us human. Life gives us lots of experiences, and for each of those experiences comes very different emotions.

We can be happy, sad, angry, frustrated, bored, fearful – the list goes on. It's important to learn strategies to help us through some of those unpleasant emotions such as anger and sadness.

When you're feeling various emotions, it's important to check in with yourself and recognise it. If you're happy, name it. Say to yourself, "I feel happy and it feels so good to be happy". If you're feeling sad and angry, name those emotions too so you can process what you're feeling. The use of affirmations may help. You may say, "I'm sad and angry because of ... but I know that it won't last".

Breathe through negative emotions, allow yourself to feel them and know that tomorrow is a new day, a day to start fresh.

Just getting through the day is sometimes enough to shake up those times when we feel crappy.

Have you been teary or stressed and no matter what you do, you just can't seem to shake it off? There is something magical about the beauty of sleep and the wonderful healing it provides.

There are times when you need the advice and support of a health care professional so never be afraid to seek support when your emotions become too overwhelming. The Kids Helpline (open 24/7) is a great resource. If ever needed, you can give them a call on 1800 55 1800.

Doing what you can to make safe and healthy choices to get to through the day is enough. Try going for a walk or taking a nice warm shower or bath.

As the sun sets, all that has happened that day is in the past.

Tomorrow is a new day, a new opportunity to start your day right and work towards creating your day and life, just the way you want it.

> *When times get tough, I know I have the skills and resources to help get through these times. I choose to do things that bring me comfort and I breathe through the ups and downs of my emotions, knowing this will pass.*

Breathing Techniques

When you're stressed or angry, try this simple breathing technique that may help pass the time and get through the tough times.

Sit or lay down comfortably.

Take a deep breath in through your nose, counting slowly.

Hold it for a few seconds. Choose a number, five, seven etc.

Breathe out as you slowly count to your number.

Repeat.

Once you've finished the breathing exercises, start with some positive affirmations and be your biggest support to get you through those tough times.

You've got this!

> *I take a deep breath in and I hold it in. I breathe out slowly. I repeat this technique until I feel a sense of calm. Sometimes I just need to slow down and take a few deep breaths.*

Positive Friendships

Friendships are important and can be the most significant connection in your teens. Friendships can also create tricky situations when relationships become unsettled, or there are disagreements or issues between friendship groups. Healthy and lasting friendships take effort and must balance trust, care and compassion from both sides.

It's important to understand the social connection and all the awesome things friends do for us.

Friends provide a sense of belonging. Hanging with like-minded people who understand us gives a great sense of comfort. Our friends also provide emotional support and can help us navigate many ups and downs.

It's essential to select your circle of friends wisely and surround yourself with people who support and uplift you.

Positive friendships can contribute to increased happiness, self-esteem, and overall wellbeing so be sure to finds yourself some nice friends who uplift and inspire you to be the best version of yourself.

I attract healthy and positive friendships into my life.

The Change Starts Now

There is no better time than now. Commit to the change you want to see in your life.

Remember that time waits for no one. It is never too late to start something new. You may want to utilise the Dream Big Journal to help get your dreams and goals out of your head and onto paper – that is the first step. As you progress, it's amazing to watch them manifest into reality.

Remember, the only person who can stop you is you.

It's important to reflect on those limiting beliefs and continue the positive self-talk to help you stay focused. Know that you are worthy of this change. You have attracted it into your life.

The change starts now. I'm ready for this change. Today is a new day to start fresh. I'm not limited by my past beliefs. I use positive self-talk to help me stay focused and know that I can do anything I set my mind to.

Have a Positive Attitude

A positive attitude creates a more pleasing personality for others to connect with. There are many layers to what having a positive attitude means. It could mean that you bring joy and positivity wherever you go.

Here are some words that we feel describe a positive person: joyful, calm, energetic, caring, kind, responsive, confident, approachable, honest, trustworthy, uplifting - the list goes on. Consider what a positive attitude means to you and list the qualities you like and want to work on.

Positivity is uplifting. Try to bring joy and positive vibes wherever you go. Don't waste your time engaging with the low vibe or negative energy. Be the sunshine and light wherever you can.

*I enjoy being around positive people
and I'm a joy to be around.
I'm continuing to work on being my best self.*

Stay Focused on Your Dreams

Start your day right and focus on your dreams. Staying focused on what and where you give your energy is essential. What you watch or do first thing in the morning can prime your brain to absorb and accept a particular state for the rest of the day. For example, waking up every morning and watching TikTok could be beneficial if you dream of holding the record of watching the most TikTok's or if you dream of creating content and building a career around TikTok. If this doesn't apply to your dreams and goals, it is most likely not moving you closer to your vision.

How disempowering would it be to look back and to have never turned your life in the direction you wanted to?

Many successful people do things to help them be successful. It's great to learn from those who are smashing through their goals. You'll find that many successful people implement things like visualising, journaling, gratitude, or mindfulness into their daily practice to help them stay focused on their dreams. Try a few things and see what works for you. Share with others or even us as we're always trialling and adding new things into our toolkit.

> **"The biggest adventure you can take is to live the life of your dreams."**
> – Oprah Winfrey

Managing Stress

Try to recognise when you're feeling stressed or are triggered. Take yourself out of the environment and try a few techniques that may work for you. The breathing technique mentioned earlier is a great one. It's free and available everywhere. Being intentional with your breath is said to reduce stress. Try a stress ball, walk a dog, exercise, phone a friend or whatever works for you.

> *I breathe deeply and work through moments of stress. I know there are people who can help and that this will pass. I focus on the things that bring me joy.*

Passion and Purpose

Passion is the reason you may embark on something you enjoy. Purpose is the reason you're doing it. You've heard those two words a lot throughout this book. You may not even know what your passion or purpose is; however, we've given you a few things to think about in the hope of helping you find your passion and purpose.

Knowing yourself and who you really are is passion; doing something with it is purpose. It may take time to find it.

You could start to think about the things that you get most excited about. Is there a cause or something that ignites something within you? You could be passionate about sports, dancing, music, makeup, art, or helping people.

Can you pursue a career doing something you are passionate about?

Can you connect with others who have those same passions and interests?

You might not have all the answers right away; however, with time, we hope you will find your passion and purpose.

We wrote this book as part of our passion and purpose.

I may not know what my passion and purpose is but I am working on finding it. I embrace opportunities to do the things that bring me joy.

The Power of Forgiving

Forgiving is a tough one, especially when people have upset or hurt you. If there are small things in your life either at home or with friends, it can be empowering to forgive and let go of what you don't need to carry with you. What it often does is allow the anger and other emotions to be bottled up. Sometimes, it's easier to simply say "I forgive you" and let it go.

It doesn't mean that you need to forget but you can choose forgiveness to free up some of the anger or resentment you may be carrying.

We know this is not easy particularly when someone has really upset you. You may find some techniques that work well for you. All we know is that from our experience, carrying that anger within us simply makes us feel no good. We must find a way to let it go to release the stress that we're holding within our body.

*I may forgive and I may choose to forget.
I try not to hold on to anger and sadness
so I can truly be my best.*

Accepting Support

You don't have to do it all on your own. All the great people you admire, your heroes, your idols, they built themselves on the shoulders of the people who came before them. There is always someone who can help. Reach out if and when you get stuck.

Remember, there is no shame in asking for support. You don't have to do it alone. Is there something you've been struggling with and are too afraid to ask for help? Brainstorm and think of a few trusted people or even just one person who can support you.

I am not afraid to ask for help when needed.

Growing Your Confidence

Confidence is an important skill to always work on, even into your adult years. Some people look as though they ooze confidence, but let's face it, there are many who suffer with low confidence when it comes to stepping out of their comfort zone.

When you feel your confidence is shot and you're feeling overwhelmed with life, ask yourself why you're feeling that way. Think about people who you admire how they would approach the situation.

Take a deep breath and remind yourself that challenging yourself and your abilities may allow you to grow and develop, even in tough times.

Challenge your inner critic, and watch your confidence and self-esteem grow.

It's like a muscle. We must use it to continue to grow our confidence by challenging ourselves to be strong, even in those times where we don't feel like we can do it.

Remember, everyone is a person just like you. Try your best to overcome limiting beliefs, put your shoulders back, stand tall and be you. You are amazing!

I am a magnet for positive experiences.
I find new ways to grow my confidence.
I stand tall knowing that I am good enough and smart enough to do whatever I set my mind to.

Say Yes to Opportunities

There will be times throughout your teens where you'll be asked if you want to participate in certain experiences or opportunities.

While the safest thing to say is no, we encourage you to say yes to opportunities as you never know what doors may open, what you may learn or who you may meet from the experience. With practice, you may begin to feel more confident when saying yes to opportunities and challenging yourself to get outside your comfort zone.

You can do it… say YES!

I say yes to opportunities that may open doors or allow me to learn and grow.

Choose Your Thoughts Wisely

Monitor your thoughts. Sometimes we just need to bring ourselves back to the present moment when our mind starts to drift off, and our thoughts are spiralling out of control.

A simple strategy is to say to yourself "be present" or "be aware". This is important when fearful or stressful thoughts enter our minds.

At times, we do the 'add on' method where we keep adding to the negative or stressful thoughts. This allows the stress or fear to build in our minds which adds to our stress and anxiety levels.

When stressful or negative thoughts enter your mind, take a deep breath, and say, "Let it go", or try some positive affirmations such as, "I am safe", "This will pass". Get out and try to shake it up. A simple walk or some fresh air is a good strategy to disrupt unhelpful thoughts.

> "Whatever the mind
> can conceive and believe,
> it can achieve."
> – *Napoleon Hill*

Should'ves, Could'ves and Would'ves Don't Count

There's nothing worse than thinking back on occasions where you felt like you should have said yes to an opportunity. Learn from these FOMO experiences. Life is constantly presenting new experiences and opportunities. Don't let fear hold you back and make up excuses as to why you shouldn't do something, especially if there is a possibility that it may bring you joy or open doors for learning and growth. Take each opportunity with both hands, dive in, and give it a go. You'll never know unless you try.

> *I think deeply about the decisions I make even though sometimes things may scare me. If there's an opportunity to learn or grow, I step into this space with an open*

heart. I don't want to look back and wish I would have said yes to that opportunity. I say yes to learning and growing.

Be Your Own Biggest Cheerleader

If you don't have anyone to cheer you on or encourage your dreams and goals, you have you – the most amazing person you know! Back yourself and praise your achievements and cheer yourself on with positive self-talk and affirmations. We all need a champion, but sadly, sometimes we need to be a champion for ourselves. Encourage yourself and take the time to think about your achievements. Tell yourself that you are proud and don't allow the negative thoughts or ideas from others stop you from working towards your dreams and goals.

I am proud of myself and I'm always working towards my dreams and goals.
I am my own biggest cheerleader and I am proud of who I am and all I'm working towards.

The Power of You

Everyone is different and unique. We all have various upbringings, support networks and privileges, and there are certain things that we can't change. We are all human, and jealousy and comparing ourselves with others is in our nature. When you feel upset about your opportunities or home life, bring your mind back to yourself and what's in your control. Remember that everyone can achieve greatness. Some of the most influential and successful people have had complicated lives. The lesson here is that it doesn't matter where we were born, what our home life is like, or what champions we have. We are human and can make something out of any situation. Focus on you and your dream of living your best life.

I love myself, just the way I am.
I focus on my dreams and living my best life.

Be Kind to Yourself

Cursing and criticising ourselves is not good. We're often the first to blame ourselves if we make a mistake. Remember that you're only human and that practising kindness to yourself and others is essential. Watch your thoughts and words and interrupt any self-criticism. Remember to be kind if you hear yourself calling yourself names or focusing on the negatives. We all make mistakes, and even when we have messed up, there is always room to learn and grow, so be kind and show yourself some love and compassion.

> *I am kind. I forgive and show the same respect, love and compassion to myself as I show to others.*

YOLO

You Only Live Once (YOLO) is a term many teens use. Some think it means to be reckless. It's a term that we should take seriously. We should make the most of life and not waste opportunities to tap into our potential and be our best.

I only live once and I'm going to make the most of the opportunities I have. I don't waste my time and energy on things that don't serve me.

Your Legacy

What is the legacy that you want to leave behind?

Do you want to be someone that made a difference in the lives of others?

Do you want to be remembered as someone who was brave and resilient?

There are endless opportunities to do good in this world.

What do you want to do?

What do you want to achieve?

Importantly, how will you feel when you've achieved your dreams and goals?

I am me. There is no one like me. There are endless opportunities to do good, and I want to live a life where I can be remembered for all the amazing things I have achieved and the difference I've made.

Breathe and Shake it Up

Move your body, breathe deeply and shake it up.

If you're feeling stressed or overwhelmed, don't stay inside and let it sit with you.

Try getting out and going for a walk around the block or to the local park.

Look out on the horizon and reflect on how truly blessed you are.

Think about others around the world who may not have access to this peace and safety. Take a deep breath in and hold it. Focus on the area where you feel anxiety and then let it go.

These times are only temporary and will be sure to pass.

I take a deep breath shake up the energy I don't need. I let it go.

Learn to Love Yourself

Know that you are unique and beautiful in your own way. How boring would this world be if we were all the same? Love every part of who you are.

Limiting beliefs and lack of self-love prevent us from seizing the moment and engaging in that feeling of love. In order to fully love others, we also need to learn to love ourselves. Look in the mirror and acknowledge and give love to every part of your body. Think about your organs, your skin, your eyes, every part of your body that makes up you. Give love and express gratitude as you are beautiful and unique.

There is no one like you!

I love every part of my healthy body and mind. I express gratitude for I am beautiful and unique.

Toxic Gossip

We may like to vent when others annoy us, but we must remember that there are more important and positive things we can choose to focus our energy on. Sometimes, the more we focus on things that annoy us, the more they annoy us. It can be like adding fuel to the fire. Try redirecting your energy and choosing to talk about more positive things. Gossiping and giving power to what others are doing or not doing takes your focus and energy away from you, and your main priority is YOU!

I speak kind and positive words.

Quick Reads to Inspire and Motivate

Coping With Stress

Life can sometimes throw unexpected challenges our way, and taking care of ourselves is essential, especially when stress takes its toll.

Watch something funny, phone a supportive friend, push yourself to go for a walk, or even treat yourself to extra sleep.

Know that the tough times don't last and that we don't always have to be happy.

Ride the waves, and it shall soon pass.

*Life may not be easy.
When obstacles come my way,
I think carefully about how I respond.
I take care of myself and do things
that make me feel good.*

Express Gratitude Daily

Saying THANK YOU is extremely powerful and has a magical way of shifting your focus to the positive things in your life. Think about all the little things that you're thankful for and express gratitude and appreciation for them. You may start to notice more things that you're grateful for, and your energy may shift, creating a more positive and optimistic version of yourself. The law of attraction states that the more we are grateful, the more the Universe will send us things to be grateful for. There's no harm in expressing gratitude and having a more positive outlook on life. A positive mind is a magnet for positive experiences.

I take time to think about the things that I'm grateful for. Whilst there is so much I want or may not have, I know there are an abundance of things that I can express gratitude for.
Thank you – thank you – thank you.

Everyone Makes Mistakes

We all mess up sometimes. If you've made a mistake, accept it, apologise and move on. Everyone makes mistakes, and it's okay to admit if you've made one. Don't ever be afraid of admitting you are wrong. No one is perfect, and the word sorry is there for a reason.

I forgive myself when I make mistakes. I'm not afraid to admit when I have made a mistake. If I make a mistake, I learn from it and try not to make the same mistake twice.

Being Kind Can Save and Change Lives

Nick Vujicic was born with no arms and no legs and has found his resilience despite his challenges. He is now an author, speaker, husband and father.

Nick shared a story about an experience from primary school where kids would say mean things about his appearance. He felt different, and the kids around him took every opportunity to let him know how different he was.

He shared a story about a day at school when he had been bullied continuously throughout the day. He counted the number of times kids said mean things. With each comment, his confidence and self-worth slowly drained away. He said to himself that if he received one more negative comment, he wouldn't be returning to school – he was ready to give up. He was sad and defeated and didn't want to continue with the constant harassment and bullying.

While leaving the school grounds in his wheelchair, he heard a girl call out, "Hey Nick!" He thought to himself, "This is it. This is going to be the one." To his surprise, she said, "I just want to let you know you're looking good today".

He left feeling happy, and suddenly, his fear and anxiety melted away.

That little girl made his day.

Be kind and compassionate as you never know what someone else is going through. It doesn't hurt to give a compliment and say something nice to someone – you just may make their day or change their life.

> *Compliments and kindness can change someone's life. I choose to be kind by finding ways to uplift and bring out the best out of others. I'm mindful of the words that I speak and the impact they may have on others.*

Get Out of Your Comfort Zone

Getting out of our comfort zone and trying new things is difficult for many of us. Things such as trying a new sport, meeting a new group of people or even trying things like surfing, zip lining, high ropes or dancing can be scary at first; however, if you try, you may like or even love it. So give new things a go and allow yourself to be vulnerable and courageous.

Go through life with an open mind, knowing that many experiences just may bring us happiness – that thing we're all chasing.

> *I'm prepared to try new things. Life is meant for living. I am courageous and will always make smart and calculated decisions about my health and safety. I embrace opportunities to get out of my comfort zone when needed.*

Now is Your Time to Shine

Shine like no one is watching. Work towards living the life of your dreams. Break the cycle and be the change you want to see.

Move towards your dreams and goals with strength and courage. Take ownership of where you are heading and how you will get there. Acknowledge that no one else can do the work for you. Success takes courage and continuous motivation.

> "Nothing can dim the light which shines from within."
> – Maya Angelou

Focus on Happiness

We don't need money or material things to be happy. Look at people around the world. Some are from our most disadvantaged, and the poorest communities are sometimes the happiest. They appreciate the little things. If you were not born with an abundance of love, resources, and happiness, it doesn't necessarily mean that you can't have those things. Think about what you need or want and, make a plan and go get them.

My past and experiences of yesterday do not direct my future today.

We All Have a Story

We all have a story and are yet to write the rest of our story. Know that everyone is going through something, despite what you may see on social media or what they share. Focus on your story and the difference you can make. Your story is waiting for it to be written or to be re-written. You are the author of your story; you choose the next chapter and what you want to do, what you want to achieve and who you want to be. Your story makes you YOU, and it is unique and wonderful. Use your story for good.

> **"You are the author of your story and the writer of your dreams."**
> – Kylie Captain

Blaming Does Not Help

Don't blame others for your circumstances. Blaming doesn't help get us from where we are to where we need to be. Reflect on the power of YOU. What can you do to make the positive changes you want to see? It's easy to become stuck and give up when we allow resentment to settle in. Blaming others for our circumstances may only cause us sadness so it's important to only focus on the things that we can change.

I listen, I learn, and every day, I am becoming a better version of myself.

Find a Champion

We encourage you to seek out someone who believes in you, someone who sees your potential, someone you can share your hopes and dreams with. Ask for guidance and keep an eye out for the signs; there is someone out there for everyone. Call them a mentor, a friend or coach and value their support and guidance. Maybe you can even become a mentor for others by guiding and leading the way. There is always someone to help. Open your heart and mind to the possibilities and find your person.

**"It's never a failure
if you learn something from it."**
– Ashley Hetherington

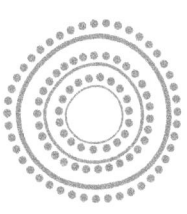

Find Your Courage

Nelson Mandela once said, *"It always seems impossible until it's done"*.

Every new journey is hard; however, you will never know if you will succeed unless you try.

We encourage you to take that leap of faith, believe in yourself and be courageous.

Look at yourself in the mirror and tell yourself you're good enough. Go and achieve whatever you dream of and more.

I am good enough and I am smart enough. I work towards my dreams with courage and determination.

Believe That You Matter

Are you good at giving advice to others?

We're often great friends and have lots of helpful advice to give.

However, when we need help, we often don't give our circumstances the same thought and attention.

When you face challenges and are unsure what to do, imagine what you're experiencing is that of a friend.

What advice would you give them?

What would you tell them to start doing and stop doing?

Believe that you matter just as much or more than anyone else in your life.

> *I am strong and resilient. I use my experiences to help and support others and also to help and support myself.*

Heal, Learn and Grow

Find strength in reflecting on all the things that you're grateful for and heal and grow from past challenges.

Ask yourself, "What is the lesson all of my experiences have taught me?"

In the words of Dr Seuss, remember:

"You have brains in your head.
You have feet in your shoes.
You can steer yourself any direction you choose. You're on your own.
And you know what you know.
And YOU are the one who'll decide where you go... Oh, the places you'll go!"

> **"The best way to predict your future is to create it."**
> *– Abraham Lincoln*

Live a Life of Positivity

Remind yourself to be positive. Speak nice words and be optimistic.

Remember that good things come to good people, and that you deserve positive people and experiences in your life.

When you learn, share this knowledge with others, too.

Your positivity can truly help many. Be the sunshine and the light for all with your positive energy.

I bring my positive energy wherever I go.

Focus on Good Health

If there's an area in your body that you want to improve, the best place to start is to focus on all the areas that work well and those you're grateful for.

Start by writing a list of all the things you are thankful for.

Give thanks for your working legs that get you around each day or your eyes that allow you to see and experience life.

Remember that many people would give anything to have what you have.

If there is any area in your body that you want to improve, start by expressing gratitude for what you have.

Close your eyes, visualise your improved health, and make healthy living your priority.

Nurture and care for your body.

I give thanks for my body and the good health that I have. There are many people who would love to have what I have. I focus on my health and express gratitude for my healthy mind and body.

Healthy Relationships

To attract healthy relationships with friends, family members or other special people in your life, you should focus on their strengths. Start by giving thanks for all the things you appreciate about them. The more you concentrate on the positives and what you enjoy most about others, the more you notice their strengths. In turn, they may start seeing yours, and your relationships may begin to improve. It's human nature to thrive on encouragement and positivity.

Find it in your heart to focus on their strengths and appreciate the healthy relationships in your life.

Set high expectations for the relationships you desire.

Notice the good in people and tell them you appreciate them. Lead by example and treat people how you want to be treated. Use your high vibe positivity and attract positive and healthy relationships.

> *I surround myself with positive*
> *people and value healthy and*
> *positive relationships.*

Believe in Your Ability

Use your imagination and dream big and believe in your ability. You can achieve your goals by first creating and dreaming up what you want to achieve.

You can apply the same principles to many other areas in your life. Always remember that if somebody else can learn something or do something, then so can you.

We are only limited by our imagination and the belief in our ability to succeed.

Even though our dreams may scare us, we can't let life and opportunities pass us by.

Life is about living and continuously reflecting on where we are and where we want to be.

It's never too late to start something new.

> **"Education is the passport to the future, for tomorrow belongs to those who prepare for it today."**
> – Malcolm X

Helping and Inspiring Others

How good does it feel when we are able to help someone?

Research shows that when learning new information, by teaching someone else, it helps us absorb the information and learn.

Find yourself a buddy or someone who you feel could use some positivity in their life.

Share some of the things you have learnt. Don't be embarrassed about dreaming big and making change.

You may inspire others, too. They may admire your strength and courage, and you may help them create positive change.

Lead by example, and as you learn and grow, help others too.

I work towards my dreams and goals, and I enjoy helping others too.

Goal Setting and Journaling

Journaling is an amazing tool for goal setting.

Start by writing your thoughts about the goals you're hoping to achieve. Some prompts could include short-term and long-term goals and what you're going to start doing to achieve them.

You'll find prompts at the back of this book. Write them down and highlight your favourite quotes or tips.

When setting goals, it's important to think about what you're going to stop doing as well as the people you need to spend more time with.

Think about your ultimate goal if there was no chance of failing.

Once you've set your goals, you may even want to share them with a friend or mentor.

Write your goals as if you've already achieved them.

For example, write a letter to your future self, looking back and reflecting on how proud you are for sticking to your plan.

Get excited and describe your feelings as if you have already achieved your goals.

Having our goals written down is a powerful thing that is difficult to understand until you start the process.

Just putting pen to paper is an extremely therapeutic exercise. You can write about how you're feeling, something that's frustrating you, or things you're grateful for.

Give it a go and see for yourself. 😊

> **"A little progress each day
> adds up to big results."**
> – *Satya Nani*

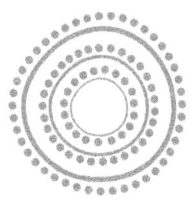

Vision Boards

Vision boards are fun and can be transformational. They help keep our dreams alive by reminding us why we started. They are also a great help when self-doubt creeps in.

It's also a deadly exercise that you can do with friends or family. You can even create digital vision boards in a few minutes on Canva. The hands-on boards are our favourite. All you need is some magazines or pictures and quotes from the internet, a frame or corkboard, scissors, stickers and pencils.

Be creative and add everything you're dreaming of, along with inspirational quotes and messages to help you stay motivated.

I enjoy bringing my visions to life.

The Power of Visualisation

Visualisation and manifesting are a crucial part of the dreaming process.

The Secret by Rhonda Byrne explains that the magic is in creating a movie in your mind about what you want to achieve. Close your eyes and visualise the result of what you're dreaming up. Don't think about everything you need to do to get there. You've already done that.

Don't think about the process and all the hurdles you need to get through along the way, fast-forward till the end. Visualise the phone call when you've been told that you were successful. See yourself jumping up and down with joy and excitement. You can also visualise telling someone the great news. Feel all the feelings as if you've already achieved it. Remember to always say thank you!

When things don't work out there is always a lesson to be learnt from the process.

Everything happens for a reason.

> "The future belongs to those who believe in the beauty of their dreams."
> – Eleanor Roosevelt

Positive Self-Talk

We all need positivity in our lives.

You may like to incorporate positive self-talk or use positive quotes as a way to help you set goals, and stay motivated. It's a simple process where you can be creative in the process by coming up with your own beautiful quotes and inspiring messages.

Believe in yourself and set out on a journey of living your best life.

> *I am smart, capable, and I am a powerful creator of my dreams.*

Select Your Circle

It may be helpful to have an accountability group or someone who is aware of your goals who can check in with you.

You may even want to join a positive Facebook group where you may find a community of people who uplift and inspire you.

Having someone who is aware of your goals can be a great way to help you stay committed and motivated.

Remember to choose someone who makes you feel good and brings out the best in you.

Choose your circle wisely. Replace the negative people with those make you feel good and want to see you win.

> I surround myself with people who uplift and inspire me. I enjoy being around those who help me be my best.

Move Your Body

Spending just ten minutes in the morning engaging in some form of exercise can dramatically improve your life.

Find ways to move your body.

Exercise is good for both our body and mind.

If you can, join a gym, a class, or even go for a walk. If none of that is for you, then hit the floor and do some stretches or pilates strength exercises.

There are lots of short instructions on YouTube. Movement can be transformative and help in many areas of life. Moving helps us stay strong, physically and mentally and may be the thing that can helps us get through tricky times,

Give it a go and get moving and towards your dreams and goals.

> "If you fail to plan, you plan to fail."
> – Benjamin Franklin

Ride the Waves of Live

Life has its ups and downs. We hope we'll experience mostly ups, but, at times there may be downs. Sometimes this may come in the form of grief which is something that may come into your life and turn your world upside down. Sometimes the downs may take us away from our dreams and goals. Remember, life may get rocky, but soon there will be smoother seas ahead.

I ride the waves of life. At times things get rocky, however I know soon enough there will be smoother seas ahead.

Fear of Judgement

Fear of judgment often stops many people from pursuing their dreams and goals. Don't let this be you. Be brave and work through any fear that may creep in.

Being the first to embark on a new career or study opportunity can be scary as we often worry too much about what others think. Be aware of the fear and challenge it. You can be the first and do anything your heart desires. Don't let others choose your path. You do you and decide on the life and future you want.

Fear and judgement does not hold me back. I take control of my life and work towards my dreams and the life I desire.

Drugs and Alcohol

There may be times when you are faced with peer pressure or the temptation to experiment with drugs and alcohol. While many would say that's what teens do, that isn't always the case. There are many adults out there who have never touched drugs or alcohol, and even some who have been surrounded by it their entire lives.

We encourage you to make smart and make wise choices for yourself. Don't give in to peer pressure and do things just because those around you are doing them.

There are many tragedies and horrible things that happen to people when under the influence of drugs and alcohol. Many of these things could be accidental. Some drink too much and fall over and hurt themselves or act aggressively and get into trouble and even land themselves in prison.

Some have fun when drinking or taking drugs but wake up feeling vulnerable and regretting decisions they made while under the influence.

While the high of drugs and alcohol may be fun temporarily, the next day and following days could be full of anxiety.

There are many things you need to consider. Weigh up the pros and cons. Drugs and alcohol may bring short-term pleasure and fun; however, at times, come with heavy consequences.

You don't have to be under the influence to have a good time. You can bring the joy and be your true, in control and authentic self to any situation. Be you!

Be wise and make smart and safe choices.

I make smart choices and always put my health and safety first.

Breaking Unhealthy Habits

You may have found yourself in a situation where you have been caught in a habit that is leading to an unhealthy lifestyle.

It could be smoking, vaping, drinking, using drugs, addiction to gaming, etc – the list goes on.

Whatever it is that you're experiencing, or perhaps a friend may be experiencing, know that change is possible with the right help and support.

Never be afraid to contact someone for help.

You may like to discuss things with a close friend at first and then find the courage to reach out to a professional or school counsellor. Some services, such as Beyond Blue and others, can help you if you're feeling down or find yourself in a vicious or negative cycle.

It's important to remember that many people experience these types of problems, and many also recover from them. If you've tried many times, that's okay; there is always a chance to start again.

Think about all of the great things you could achieve and how you may feel if you were to make that positive change.

You could have more money, feel healthier, happier, have more energy and not carry this heavy burden. Whatever it is that you might've found yourself engaging with, kick the habit and make some positive and wise choices, and put your health and wellbeing first.

Reflect on a few goal setting prompts at the back of this book and break them down with the steps you need to take to work towards those your positive goals.

Thinking about things that could get in the way is also essential. Are there people or events that may sabotage your good intentions? Planning for things that could derail you and take you off track is vital for success.

You've got this!

> *There are times when I may engage in unhealthy habits, however, I know I have the skills to make the positive change I wish to see.*

Stay Connected to Who You Really Are

Think about who you are as a person, as a family member, a community member, your morals and values.

What are the things you're proud of?

What makes you YOU?

Think of times when people have acknowledged you for your commitment or dedication to something.

Close your eyes and see yourself shining and doing the things you love.

Really connect with your deepest desires and the person you want to be. You may want to be a singer, a dancer, a sporting star, a doctor, or perhaps you want to travel the world – whatever it is – see yourself there and know that you are deserving of everything you desire and more.

Tell yourself you are strong, resilient, and capable of anything you set your mind to.

> "What if I fall?
> Oh, my darling, but what if you fly?"
> – Erin Hanson

No is a Complete Sentence

Saying no doesn't have to be complicated. In your teens it can be particularly hard to say no, especially when you may be the only one.

Saying no could be refusing to go somewhere you don't want to go to, refusing to engage in something that you're not comfortable with, refusing to get yourself into a dangerous situation, taking a substance or jigging school.

Be strong, and don't feel like you have to give excuses to support your decision.

No means no – be strong and confident in your decisions.

I trust my intuition. I know that it is okay to say no to things that don't feel right.

The Ups and Downs of Hormones

Oh, my gosh! Teenage years can be the worst regarding hormones and managing all of the emotions you feel. Sometimes, it may feel like a roller coaster of ups and downs as you progress through your teens. You could go through every emotion in one day where you may feel happy, sad, angry, then who knows what else. This cycle could stay on repeat. While some of this is normal, there is also help and support to manage these problematic hormones. Some over-the-counter vitamins and minerals can help balance out hormones, and even natural things you can engage in, such as walking, swimming, mindfulness and breathing exercises that can help navigate those tricky times when things get tough.

If you're finding that it's getting too out of control, don't be afraid to ask for help and seek support from a doctor or healthcare professional.

I choose to believe that there is kindness in the world. Wherever I go I know there is always someone there to help me in my journey of life.

Ditch the Negative Self-Talk

We are all guilty of criticising and beating ourselves up for things. There are times when we dramatise or overreact regarding specific situations, too. It could be something you said or done, and your mind continuously goes over the problem – beating yourself up. You may find yourself saying unkind things or criticising yourself. Know that the way to bring yourself back is through self-love and kindness. Forgive yourself if you've done something that you are not proud of. You may want to say, *"It's okay, I forgive myself; we all make mistakes"*.

> "Your dreams are only a thought away - imagine the 'what if'."
> – Kylie Captain

Be a Deadly Problem Solver

Some people get stuck in a vicious cycle of creating a problem for every solution. When you offer advice and support, they always have a problem for every solution. They often find themselves stuck in this negative cycle, constantly believing that there is no way out.

If you see these behaviours within yourself, stop and think about the best first step to improve the situation. Be kind to yourself and know there is always a solution to every problem. Look at it as a game and get creative with finding the best possible solutions.

Life may present ups and downs. Our job is to navigate them by continuing to ride the waves of life and enjoying the beautiful gifts along the way.

> I ride the waves of life and take
> every opportunity with both hands.
> I continue to find my way,
> even through the darkest storms.

The Innocence of Children

There is something beautiful about the innocence of children. Their smiles, the things they say and do and how they just cruise through life with joy and happiness without a care in the world. If you need some uplifting, go and talk to a child or even think of yourself as a child.

> If I have children in my life,
> I spend time with them and pick up
> on their beautiful positive energy.
> I close my eyes and think of a child
> or even visualise myself as a child.
> I see the innocence in children and
> fill my heart with happiness.

Be Kind

Being kind to others is a way of attracting kindness into your own life. How good does it feel when people are kind to you?

We need more kindness in the world, especially for teens. The best thing you can do for yourself and others is to be kind, even if others are unkind. The best form of retaliation is kindness. Smile and shake it off.

Think about how you can be kinder to people. Could there be an opportunity for you to practice a random act of kindness? These things don't always have to cost you money either. You could hold the door open or smile at someone. You could do something nice without expecting anything in return. By practising kindness, you show your true self and invite kindness to be returned to you. You are tapping into your strengths and developing your care and compassion for others. There really is no other way to be.

How can you be kind today?

I speak positive words and engage in positive experiences.

Value Integrity

Integrity is important. It's about always being honest to yourself and following your heart about the things you value most.

Integrity is staying true to yourself, even when people aren't watching.

This could be a simple as just doing the right thing and being accountable and respecting people, either at school, in your family or in the workplace.

Integrity is also about being reliable and practising what you preach.

Owning up to a mistake if you've made one shows real integrity.

I express myself through my own unique views of the world. I am who I am. There is no one like me.

Always Be Open to Learn

There are many ways to learn and get an education. School is important; however, you're always learning both in and out of the classroom. Have an open mind and think of all the possibilities and things you're yet to learn.

There are many ways to learn. It's important that we are given the opportunity to learn the way we know best.

You may enjoy learning by watching, while others may enjoy reading or hearing someone explain something to them.

Think about how you best learn and find the courage to talk to your teachers or support staff so they can be aware of how you best learn.

In addition to school, you can continue your learning outside the classroom by watching programs based on things that you're interested in.

If you like travel, watch documentaries on travel and see yourself there in these places and soaking up the atmosphere as if it were already yours.

Research and ask questions around areas that you're interested in or if you don't even know what you're interested in, ask people what they do in their spare time. What are the things they are watching or listening to?

Podcasts are cool too. Have you ever listened to one? They are really engaging and are a great way to learn and take your mind off things.

You can even learn by listening to music, or even have a go at writing, poetry or a short story.

> **"The beautiful thing about learning is that no one can take it away from you."**
> *– B.B. King*

Draw on the Strength of Your Ancestors

Whatever your background, remember that you come from a long line of ancestors who came before you. They faced many challenges and travelled through difficult times. War, scarcity, poverty and even trauma. Whenever you feel defeated, think about the shoulders you stand on and the strength that lies within in.

*My ancestors are always guiding me,
even in spirit. Whenever I am stuck,
I may take the time to sit and connect
with those who have gone before me.
I ask for support, advice and direction.
I am never alone.*

Show Up and Be of Service

Helping and serving others gives us incredible purpose in life. Think about ways in which you can serve others. It is a beautiful feeling to give up our time, energy, and knowledge. How can you be of service? Remember, you don't need to help everyone. Think carefully about who you can support and how you would like to show up in their lives.

I enjoy showing up and being of service. It feels good to help others and to be valued for the kindness I have for all.

Find Inspiration

Inspiration is everywhere. Look around and find inspiration in nature, in animals and from those around you. Read books, listen to podcasts, or follow a positive page on social media. If ever you feel defeated, know that there is an abundance of inspiration waiting for you to find. You may not always know where your inspiration is going to come from. Turn to a random page in a book or pick up the phone and call someone you haven't spoken to for a while. Keep putting in the work to be your best and look carefully for the inspiration that is around just waiting for you to find.

"There is no substitute for hard work."
– Thomas Edison

Know Your Worth

You are worthy of love, happiness, experiences and opportunities. You can have it all. You are worthy and deserving of everything you dream of and more. You are worth so much. We can't even begin to put a price or measure how worthy you are. You deserve an abundance of health, wealth and happiness and you should have it all.

> *My day begins and ends with gratitude. I know I'm worthy of happiness and success.*

Vulnerability

Vulnerability is being open with your story and allowing yourself to truly be you.

Vulnerability can be scary, however, it can also be the thing that connects you with others. It's about showing your emotions and being honest, despite the fears that pop in from time to time. Vulnerability is taking risks and not being ashamed of asking for help. Vulnerability can be one of your greatest strengths.

> **"Vulnerability is not winning or losing; it's having the courage to show up and be seen when we have no control over the outcome. Vulnerability is not weakness; it's our greatest measure of courage."**
> – Brené Brown

Be Generous

How can you be generous with your resources, whether it be your time, material things, or your energy? When you give generously from your heart, it's often returned to you. Gifting and being generous is a great quality to have. Are there people you could be generous to? Remember that giving and being kind to others also fills our hearts with purpose and pride.

I'm grateful for everyone who is kind and generous to me and in return, I do the same for others.

The Leader in You

Leadership does not need a title. True leaders demonstrate leadership through their actions. They aren't afraid to take action and work towards things they are passionate about. You don't have to be loud and outgoing to be a leader. Many incredible leaders are softly spoken, passionate people who do their part in the world by showing up and being of service to others.

There are many different leadership styles. Some people are bossy and need to demonstrate their authority while others lead through kindness and doing their best to bring out the best in others. They lead by example.

What leadership qualities do you have?

How can you become a leader and inspire others through your passions and interests?

> "Don't let what you cannot do interfere with what you can do."
> – John Wooden

The Power of Belief

Belief is not just a thought; it's a dynamic energy within us. Our beliefs shape our thoughts, emotions, and actions, often acting as an invisible guide that leads us on our path. Once you are committed and have an unwavering belief about your ability, backed by determination and courage, you will begin to strengthen muscles that will continue to grow. This, in turn, will add to your resilience, and you will become a pro at navigating these limiting beliefs and turning them into aspirations and dreams.

*My past does not dictate my future.
I know I can be and do whatever I desire.*

If Someone Else Can Do It, Then So Can You

Think to yourself, if they can do it, then so can I. Keep telling yourself that you are good enough to do whatever you set your mind to.

Positive self-talk is a powerful tool. Whether it's overcoming physical obstacles or issues with home life or friendships, we feel there is a solution for every problem, and it all starts with you!

> Success often does not come easy; it takes effort and continuous determination. I know that if someone else can do it then so can I.

Example Letter to Future Self

Writing a letter to your future self can be a great way to turn your dreams into reality. It helps us imagine what it would be like to achieve our goals, which can help us stay motivated. See below an example of what a letter to your future self may sound like.

This letter has been sitting in my drawer for the past three years. I remember writing it and feeling so unsure about myself. I was stressed and worried about all these things that weren't that important. I was concerned about friendships and not focusing on my future. I was giving things that don't matter too much energy.

I'm so happy now as I reflect on the last three years. I decided to back myself and have a go with my dreams and goals. I said yes to opportunities, even those that scared me, such as public speaking and trying Oz Tag for the first time. I thought about having a go at these things for quite some time but was too scared to try in case I failed.

I'm so glad that I said yes! I got up at assembly and spoke, and as scary as it was, it led me to great opportunities. I have never really been into sports, but I had a go. I now love Oz Tag and focus on my health and fitness. I haven't stopped playing, and I love it.

I plan my day and week rather than just rolling out of bed and waiting for it to happen.

I take time to relax and make sure that I get plenty of sleep to ensure I have the energy to focus on the things that are important to me.

I have many more dreams and goals that I want to work on over the next few years, such as enrolling in university to study social work and saving up money to go on a trip to LA!

I surround myself with people who uplift and inspire me.

Stand Tall and Be Proud

Stand up tall and be proud of who you are. Trick your mind into feeling confident when confidence isn't there. Draw strength from those around you and be the amazingly strong person you were born to be. Put your shoulders back and find your confidence. You are important and you are here to be seen. There is a difference that you can make and an abundance of opportunities waiting for you to explore.

I stand tall and proud and learn new ways to be confident in all I do.

Listen to Your Voice

Observe first, and then make the little changes. Learn new words and improve your confidence by speaking with different people. Try to come across as your ideal self. Your voice is powerful, and it matters. It's there as your guide to help you be your best. Speak up and let the world hear all of the wonderful things you have to say.

I listen to my voice and my inner strength. I choose my words wisely and I speak up about the things that matter to me. My voice matters.

There is No Better Time Than Now

There is no better time than now. Commit to the change you want to see in your life. Remember that time waits for no one. It is never too late to start something new.

Remember, the only person who can stop you is you. It's important to reflect on those limiting beliefs and continue the positive self-talk to help you stay focused. Know that you are worthy of this change. You have attracted it into your life.

"A person who never made a mistake never tried anything new."
– Albert Einstein

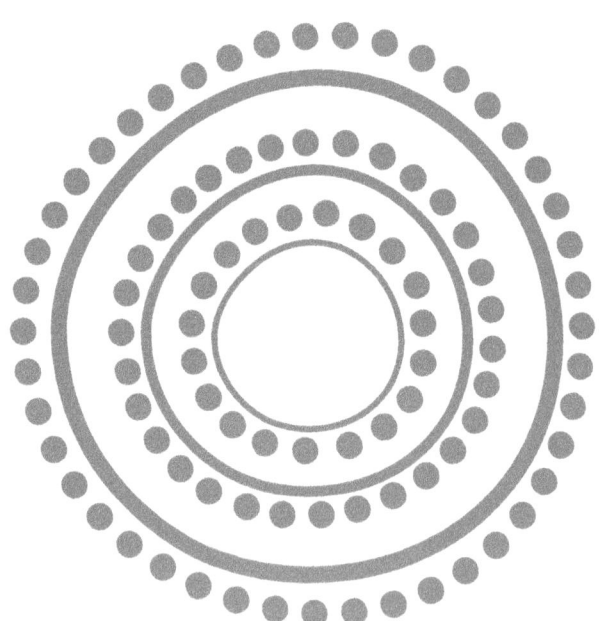

POSITIVE AFFIRMATIONS

Throughout this book, we have used an abundance of positive affirmations.

Positive affirmations are incredible and are simply positive self-talk.

Once we find our motivation and work towards positive change, particularly when out of our comfort zone, we need to stay strong and continue to tell ourselves that we can do it.

Try using positive affirmations and develop a set of affirmations that suit you and resonate with your story and journey.

The late Louise Hay was the queen of positive affirmations. They are great to write on cards or even have them as alarms on your phone to remind you of your goals and give you confidence to persevere when times get tough.

See examples below.

I choose to believe that there is kindness in the world. Wherever I go I know there is always someone there to help me in my journey of life.

I'm not perfect and no one is. I love myself the way I am. I am smart, capable, and I am a powerful creator of my dreams.

I express myself through my own unique views of the world. I am who I am. There is no one like me.

I choose my thoughts wisely. I choose my words wisely. I choose my actions wisely. I create my path through my beliefs, and the actions that I take.

I love myself today and always. I continue to surround myself with positive people.

I am open and ready to receive greatness into my life.

I trust that I am safe in this world.

Whatever comes my way, I will be ready because I'm strong and resilient.

My thoughts and actions form my reality.

I listen, I learn, and every day, I am becoming a better version of myself.

My past and experiences of yesterday do not direct my future today.

Come up with your own affirmations and have them ready to pull out of your invisible backpack that you can carry with you anywhere. If you need inspiration or are scared or unsure, don't wait for others to tell you what you must do. You have all the answers as no one knows you like you.

Affirmation for Guidance

I am protected and continuously being guided. I express gratitude for every blessing in my life. Please send me the people, circumstances and events to show me the way. I am strong and resilient, and I am ready to be the best I can be. Thank you for my guidance.

Affirmation for When Afraid

I'm safe and I seek out those who make me feel safe and protected. I am grateful for the safety in my life. We live in a safe and abundant country. I know where to go and who to call if I'm unsafe and afraid. I am grateful for my safety – I am safe, I am safe, I am safe.

Affirmation for Attracting Supportive Friends

I attract happy and positive friends into my life. Thank you for sending me incredible people and experiences for me to share my days with. I'm forever grateful for the amazing friends in my life.

Affirmation for Productivity

I'm productive and organised. I'm grateful for my ability to multitask and complete challenging things with these. Thank you for my power and for my ability to achieve greatness.

Affirmation for Better Sleep

I value my time resting and sleeping. My mind is at ease, and I sleep peacefully. Thank you for my safe, warm bed, allowing me to nourish my mind and body. I take long, deep breaths and allow myself to relax and have quality, uninterrupted sleep.

Affirmation for Healthy Relationships

I cherish and value every relationship in my life. I am happy and grateful for the wonderful people who are in my circle. I select only those who bring me joy and add value to my life. Thank you for sending me the wonderful people in my life.

Affirmation for Money and Financial Management

Thank you for the money that flows into my life to allow me to purchase things I love and to treat myself and others to things that bring us joy. I work for my money, and I manage it wisely.

Affirmation for Attracting a New Job

Thank you for this wonderful opportunity to learn, grow and share my knowledge with others. Thank you for the people who will support me on this journey in securing my new job.

Affirmation for Courage

I am courageous and I have the ability to handle any situation that comes my way. I listen deeply and tap into my strength and courage.

Affirmation for Academic Success

I am smart, and I can reach my full potential. I welcome inspiration, encouragement and support to help me be my best. I can and will achieve my full academic potential.

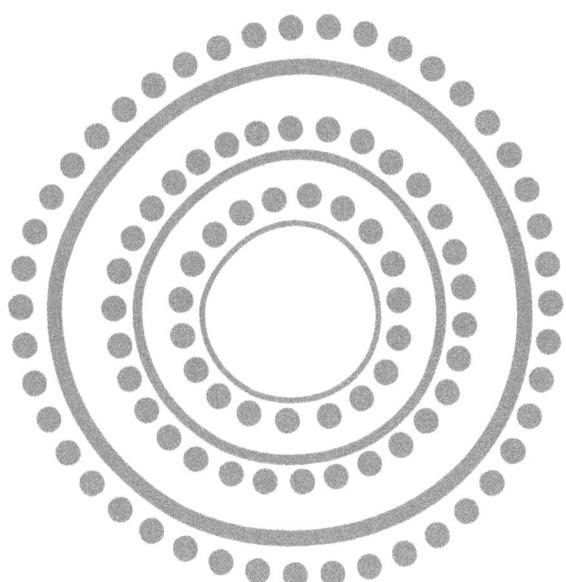

CONGRATULATIONS AND THANK YOU

Congratulations on getting to the end of the book! Thank you for allowing us to share our experiences and passion with you. We hope you've felt the love and positivity with which it was created, and importantly, we hope you've taken on a few tips and strategies to support your personal development journey.

Find your purpose and move forward with love, hope and positivity, knowing you are good enough and smart enough to do anything you set your mind to.

Take action and embark on your journey creating the life of your dreams. Remember to practice gratitude daily and really show up for life and be the best you can be.

We would love to hear from you. Please reach out and let us know your thoughts on the book and maybe something you'll start doing as a result of reading it.

We believe in you and we're proud of you.

Sending so much love and positivity your way.

Now go and dream big and create the life of your dreams.

All our love,

Kylie and Tyrell xx

> "Do the best you can until you know better. Then when you know better, do better."
>
> – Maya Angelou

DREAM BIG JOURNALING PROMPTS

I am grateful for:

....

....

....

My short-term goals:

....

....

....

My long-term goals:

....

....

....

The small steps and strategies to help me reach my goals:

....

....

....

....

The people who can help me:

....

....

....

....

The things that could get in the way:

....

....

....

I can prevent people or things sabotaging my goals by:

....

....

....

The things I admire about those who inspire me:

....

....

....

....

....

How I'll feel when I have reached my goal:

....

....

....

My ideal career:

....

....

....

....

My dream car:

....

....

....

....

My dream house looks like:

....

....

....

....

I want to travel to:

....

....

....

....

The three most important things I want to accomplish are:

◎ ....

◎ ....

◎ ....

Three things I am going to do to help me achieve my goals:

◎ ....

◎ ....

◎ ....

Three things I'm going to stop doing:

◎ ....

◎ ....

◎ ....

My positive affirmations to help me stay motivated are:

◎ ....

◎ ....

◎ ....

Fast forward to the future and visualise yourself expressing gratitude because you have achieved your goal! Write a letter or journal your excitement because you did it!

> "Learn from yesterday,
> live for today,
> hope for tomorrow."
> – Albert Einstein

Want More?

- Contact us at info@dreambigedu.com.au to book one of our inspiring talks or workshops at your school.
- Check out the website, kyliecaptain.com.au for more info.
- Keep an eye out for our online hub, where you'll have access to videos and activities based on the themes of this book to help you be your best.
- Teachers or support staff can enrol in professional learning or our accredited training.
- Purchase a copy of the Dream Big Journal.
- Download your free goal-setting tool from the website.
- Like our social media pages by searching our names or Dream Big Education Wellbeing and Consulting.

> "A dream without a plan is just a wish."
> — Katherine Paterson

ACKNOWLEDGEMENTS

We acknowledge and thank our angels and ancestors who continue to guide and comfort us in spirit, thank you for your ongoing love and protection.

There are many people we wish to thank. Firstly, you as the readers. We acknowledge you and your story. We acknowledge your strength and resilience in wanting to do and be more.

Thank you to our family and friends their support. A very special thanks to our cousin, Annelise Dixon for being our biggest cheerleader by offering words of encouragement and helping however she could. We are forever grateful for your love and support. We can't thank you all enough for all the love and encouragement throughout our writing journey.

Special thanks to the team at Ultimate 48 Hour Author and Sharon Westin for supporting us with this project and bringing this book to life.

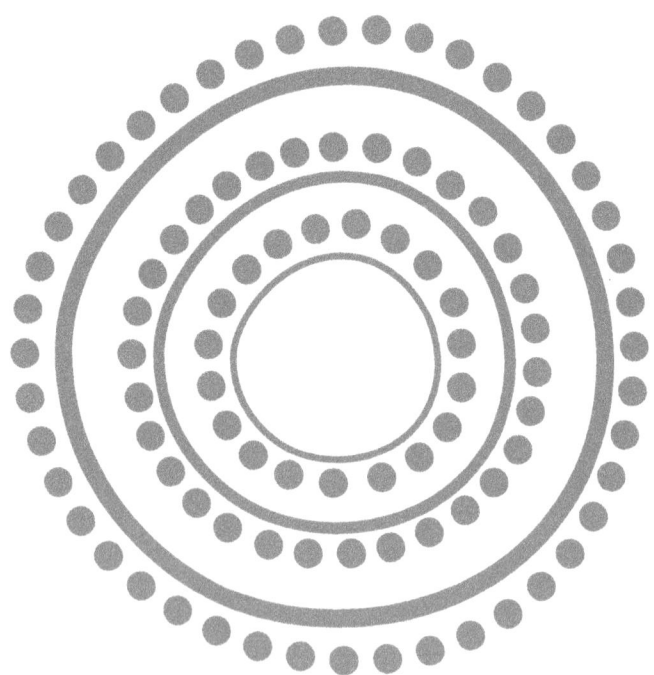

ABOUT THE AUTHORS

Tyrell Johnson

Tyrell Johnson is dedicated to empowering others through education, encouragement, and wealth-building initiatives.

With a background in supporting both the academic and wellbeing of students, he has significantly impacted the lives of many.

As an author, Tyrell has used his experiences to create positive change. His writing delves into themes that inspire personal growth, resilience, and self-discovery.

Tyrell is a Director and Facilitator at Dream Big Education Wellbeing & Consulting where he manages the business and facilitates workshops based on the topics of this book. He brings a wealth of experience from working in schools across South-West Sydney.

In addition to his writing, Tyrell has ventured into property acquisition and sales. Through his role, he actively works to build generational wealth in Aboriginal and Torres Strait Islander communities.

His journey exemplifies the transformative power of education and the potential for lasting impact through generational wealth.

About The Authors

Kylie Captain

Kylie Captain is a proud Gamilaroi woman raised in the inner-city suburbs of Redfern and Waterloo whose work has not only impacted the lives of many across Australia but has also touched readers worldwide.

In addition to this book, Kylie is the author of 'Dream Big and Imagine the What If', as well as the co-author of 'Be That Teacher who Makes a Difference'. Kylie is on a mission to make a difference.

Kylie is the Founding Director of Dream Big Education Wellbeing & Education and holds the position of President at the Aboriginal Studies Association. Kylie serves as a board director and over the past two decades, has had an impressive career, in Aboriginal education, finance and community services.

Kylie's facilitates Aboriginal cultural capability training and high-impact professional learning for teachers and leaders. Her dedication for nurturing young people is evident in her inspiring student workshops and keynote addresses nationally.

Through her writing, Kylie openly shares her personal story of loss and circumstance, revealing the inner strength and inspiration that enabled her to overcome her challenges and now live a life of freedom and choice. Along with her own grit and determination, Kylie attributes her success to the power of education and the difference a teacher made. Kylie went on to co-author her second book with that teacher, Dr Cathie Burgess.

About The Authors

Kylie's aims to use her life experiences and adversities to inspire others and have a positive impact on the lives of many – one student, one school, and one organisation at a time.

Kylie has extensive experience speaking at national conferences and events across the nation.

Contact Kylie to discuss the possibility of her speaking your school or hosting your next event.

Dream Big Education Wellbeing & Consulting is a 100% Aboriginal-owned and Supply Nation Certified national company, founded by Kylie Captain.

"Making a Difference, One Student, One School and One Organisation at a Time"

Motivational student talks and programs: As an accredited teacher and engaging and inspirational facilitator, Kylie and Tyrell facilitate inspiring author talks and goal setting workshops for students on topics including goal setting and aspirations, the power of education, wellbeing, resilience and pride in culture. Kylie is known for her Dream Big Program, an inspirational program designed to engage, inspire, and motivate students about the transformational power of education and support them in finding their hidden potential.

NESA Accredited and bespoke teacher and leadership professional development: Kylie Captain and Dr Cathie Burgess facilitate a range of empowering teacher workshops and masterclasses designed to support educators to reflect on their pedagogy and re-discover their 'why', based on the themes of her best-selling books. All workshops and masterclasses are delivered either in person or via Zoom. Where desired, sessions can be co-designed to meet the needs of the school or community, with shorter sessions available for staff meetings and

'Twilight sessions'. Topics include: curriculum and research, leading Aboriginal Education with passion and purpose, building authentic relationships with Aboriginal students and communities, teacher wellbeing, embedding culturally appropriate and localised resources and establishing culturally safe schools and learning environments.

Cultural capability training: Delivered by Kylie Captain, a highly engaging and experienced facilitator who brings a wealth of knowledge and lived experience to each session. Each session is tailored to the group or organisation and can support Reconciliation Action Plans and developing culturally safe workplaces. Sessions are thought-provoking and, at times, an emotional experience for participants as they engage in truth-telling by unpacking Aboriginal histories and cultures and learning about Australia's rich and beautiful cultures. Through her delivery, Kylie shares personal yarns and takes participants on a journey of developing empathy, leaving them wanting to learn and do more to move towards a more united and inclusive nation.

NOTES

Create The Life Of Your Dreams In Your Teens

Notes

Notes

www.ingramcontent.com/pod-product-compliance
Lightning Source LLC
Chambersburg PA
CBHW041135110526
44590CB00027B/4027